GROWING UP

Limiting Adolescence in a World Desperate for Adults

BY FRANK C. STRASBURGER

Copyright © 2012 by Frank C. Strasburger
First Edition – April 2012

ISBN
978-1-77097-556-9 (Hardcover)
978-1-77097-557-6 (Paperback)
978-1-77097-558-3 (eBook)

The cover photo is by Dylan Burrill of the United Kingdom and has been authorized for use by the author.

Published by:

FriesenPress

Suite 300 – 852 Fort Street
Victoria, BC, Canada V8W 1H8

www.friesenpress.com

Distributed to the trade by The Ingram Book Company

TABLE OF CONTENTS

Dedicated to

Carrie, Taylor, Hilary, Justin, and Rebekah,

who continue to teach me about growing up,

as well as to all those others

—and you are legion—

who have permitted me to join you on the journey.

Introduction

Growing Up is about what it means to be an adult and how our misconceptions of adulthood often lead us to aim for the wrong benchmarks. I had intended to write for parents, educators, and others involved in raising young people, as well, of course, as young people themselves. But the many engaging conversations I've had on the subject over the last year have helped me realize that, whether you're in your twenties, middle-aged, recently retired, or an octogenarian, you're probably wondering how, when, and whether you've become an adult.

So as an Episcopal priest, what do I know about growing up? I consider myself an expert in precisely nothing. Oh, yes, some people treat clergy as though we were experts, but experts are people who know nearly everything about something; I know a fair amount about a lot of things, but I don't know everything about anything, and I may not know any more about the subject of this book than you do. What I am is a consummate generalist. It helps, perhaps, that I'm the father of two sons and a daughter, all of whom are currently in their twenties; being a parent gives one a front-row seat for the drama. And it is true that, having spent nearly half a century as a teacher and priest, I've been privileged to be invited by countless people to join them in some of the most important moments on their journeys to adulthood. Finally, at 65, I suppose I could claim to have done it myself—though as my wife more than occasionally refers to me as her fourth child, I may be treading on thin ice there.

Why, then, have I written this book, and why should you read it? To be honest, this isn't the book I originally set out to write. But when I finished my original introduction, which was full of statistics and psychological theory, I realized it hadn't been much fun to write and would certainly be no fun to read. And equally to the point, while I have the capacity to research such a book, it seemed to me that I was pretending to expertise I don't have.

What I do have is stories. Stories from my experience as an English teacher, admissions director, and chaplain in several of the nation's top independent schools, where my job was, quite explicitly, to help kids grow up. Stories from my time as a parish priest working with teenagers struggling for a sense of identity in the chasm between the children they no longer wished to be and the adults they weren't sure they were ready to become. Stories from my work as Episcopal chaplain at Princeton, where, though my parishioners were some of the most able young people in the world, they, too, wrestled, often uneasily and sometimes not so successfully, with this process of becoming adults. Stories from my tenure as founding president of Princeton in Africa, providing young people on the cusp of adulthood with the opportunity to work with some of the top service organizations in Africa, helping them sort out how their service has affected not only those they've served but also the people they themselves are in the process of becoming. Stories from my own life as the father of three bright, talented, independent, and very different children, all of them now grown, but not without the requisite dose of blood, sweat, and tears. And finally, of course, stories from my own journey to adulthood.

You, too, have stories, and I trust you will find in mine echoes of your own so that you can look at yours again from a slightly different vantage point. My purpose is not to tell you what you may well already know but, rather, to encourage you to reconsider the wisdom you've accumulated on your way to adulthood and as you, like me, have accompanied others as they've walked that path.

So that's why you should read this book. But why did I write it? Both to raise and to try to respond to four questions: What does it mean to grow up? Why does it take some people so long? Is our culture, in which adolescence or something akin to it seems sometimes endless, especially resistant to adulthood? And can we do anything about all of that?

Mary allegedly bore Jesus when she was just 13. Alexander the Great was 20 when he became king of Macedonia and 22 when he began conquering the world (although, of course, he was dead by 33). Queen Victoria ruled Great Britain at 18. By the time he was 35, Mozart was dead, having nevertheless already composed over 600 works, thus establishing himself as one of history's greatest composers. And by the time Einstein was 27, he had done most of the work that made his name the eponym of intellectual brilliance.

These are anomalies, of course. Few of us are conquering heroes, musical prodigies, or scientific geniuses. But Mary would not have been unusual in becoming a mother at 13, the same age at which, for millennia, boys became men in most human societies. Like their counterparts in the rest of the animal world, once human beings were old enough to reproduce, they began to take their appointed places in the social order. Women managed the home and took care of the young while men hunted and gathered. Even as societies became more complex and the labor to support them required more training, teens were still expected to take on the adult responsibilities of marriage, childrearing, and, wage-earning.

The separation of our psychosocial from our physical status is a relatively recent phenomenon. In 1904, psychologist and educator G. Stanley Hall introduced "adolescence" to the social vocabulary with his groundbreaking work on the subject,[1] and later psychologists like Erik Erikson helped set Hall's work in a larger context by identifying adolescence among the various stages of life. Erikson suggested that what adolescence is largely about is identity formation[2]—something that would no doubt have completely baffled Mary, though it may have at least some connection to the individualizing approach Jesus brought to Jewish faith. As difficult as it is for 21st century humans to imagine—especially those of us nurtured in democratic societies that value the individual—few people seem to have had any notion of personal identity prior to the 16th century, when the Reformation and, subsequently, the Enlightenment began to propel such ideas as individual rights, personal faith, the human psyche, and the personal unconscious.

At the same time, the rise of science on the one hand and the march of democracy on the other, along with their mutual requirement of an educated citizenry, led inexorably to formal schooling, even beyond grammar school. Secondary and tertiary education, once the domain only of the wealthy and well connected, began to take hold more universally in the second half of the 19th century in the United States and elsewhere. Whereas in 1870, only about 2% of Americans were high school graduates,[3] more than 70% are today, and more than 70% of high school graduates go on to college.[4] Even entry-level jobs in all but a few sectors of the economy require, at the least, college-level training if not an undergraduate degree; and professional careers require anywhere from one to five or more years of graduate education.

Unfortunately, all of this education may not be make us any smarter. In their troubling book, *Academically Adrift: Limited Learning on College Campuses,* Professors Richard Arum of New York University and Josipa Roksa of the University of Virginia reveal that a large proportion of students aren't really learning much at college. Measuring the analytic and problem-solving skills of more than 2300 students at a broad range of America's roughly 2000 4-year colleges, they found that 45% made no improvement during their first two years.[5] While graduates may hold the degree required for their resumes, they may not have absorbed the education that adulthood requires of their intellectual growth. But whether they've learned anything or not, the time spent in school has postponed their entry into the job market.

As dramatic a role as education has played in postponing employment, advances in birth control, changes in sexual mores, and the equalization of gender roles have similarly delayed marriage and child-bearing. Effective birth control has substantially ameliorated the age-old threat of unintended pregnancy out of wedlock, freeing women of the necessity to choose between relationship and career, and releasing both women and men from social constraints against premarital intimacy. Not surprisingly, the median age for first marriages among men has risen from just under 23 in 1960 to just over 28 in 2010, and among women from just over 20 in 1960 to just over 26 in 2010.[6]

So when, exactly, do people become adults?

Commonly, we think of functional benchmarks: permanent employment, financial independence, independent living arrangements, marriage, and parenthood. But with all of those targets delayed by a decade or more, what was once a sprint to adulthood has become a marathon. Philip Glotzbach, president of Skidmore College, observed in remarks to parents during a 2010 Parents Weekend that adolescence may last these days until age 35.

Glotzbach is hardly alone. The Future of Children, a social science research collaboration of the Woodrow Wilson School at Princeton University and the Brookings Institution, devoted the Spring 2010 issue of its journal to the "Transition to Adulthood." Articles by some of the nation's top experts on the subject argue persuasively that milestones the last generation reached by their mid-twenties are unlikely to be achieved by most current young people until their late twenties to mid-thirties. Moreover, the delay is not temporary, according to the research, but, rather, the result of economic and social trends that are going to be with us for the foreseeable future.[7]

Parents, schools, and society in general are being forced to adjust to this new stage that some have termed "extended adolescence" and others, "emerging adulthood." Whatever it's called, the elusiveness of full maturity to an increasing percentage of the population is a matter of concern. If Glotzbach's estimate is anywhere near the mark, barely half of the American people are "adults." That's just a little scary. At least as frightening—though perhaps no surprise, given the puerile nature of so much of our political life—is that, by that same estimate, fewer than 60% of registered voters are adults.[8]

Given the intimidating challenges our nation and world face, can we survive a largely adolescent populace? Can the next generation afford to wait nearly half of their lives to become adults? And if the answer to both of those questions is "No," then is there anything we can do to advance adulthood?

Fortunately, the answer to *that* question is "Yes." Part of the solution lies in identifying those aspects of adulthood over which individuals can exercise some control, as opposed to those subject to broad social or economic influences largely beyond anyone's power. Making adulthood or even identity formation entirely dependent upon financial independence, home ownership, marriage, and parenthood (all tests of adulthood, incidentally, that both Plato and Jesus would have failed) leaves young people's maturation process entirely vulnerable to the whims of the economy. More to the point, however, those benchmarks fall woefully short as measures of maturity. They may be indicators, but we all know people who can check all of those boxes and are anything but adults.

I want to propose altogether different criteria for adulthood—a definition based less on functions than on a state of being:

> We become adults when
> *we embrace the limitations of human mortality,* and
> *we understand we are not the center of the universe.*

The inevitability of death is a fact of human nature, of course, but there's more to mortality than that. Our status as mortals subjects us to a host of limits: physically, we can be in only one place at a time; we inhabit bodies which themselves are subject to the laws of physics, including entropy, which means that even as our bodies are creating new cells all the time, as creatures, we're in a continuous state of deterioration. Indeed, though it is certainly not the most optimistic way to look at life, we nevertheless can't escape the fact that we begin dying at birth.

If none of us is omnipotent, and even the most powerful of us ultimately lose our grip, then, much as most of us would like to be perennial winners, physically speaking, at least, we're headed downhill every second of every day—indeed, sooner or later for all of us, time will run out.

As small children, we dream big dreams. We haven't tested our limits and are largely ignorant of them. Our heroes live happily ever after; why shouldn't we? But to be mortal is not just to die; it is to be imperfect, and the flaws of our innate humanity inevitably spoil the childhood dream that all things are possible, that we don't have to make choices, that we can be anything and do anything we want, that we can always win—or if we begin to suspect we can't, that there must be something deeply wrong with us that doesn't afflict others.

The hardest thing for most of us about being mortal isn't that we're not going to live forever but that we have so much less control than we'd like. Our early misunderstanding as toddlers that our parents control everything leads easily to a second illusion that ultimate control lies somewhere out there for us, as well. The disintegration of both illusions is a painful but necessary step in our growing up—a step sufficiently daunting, embarrassing, and frightening that some people never take it. And it's not just our own physical limitations that deprive us of control; it's the inconvenient presence of everyone else waging their own battles for command of their destinies. Understanding that all those other people matter at least as much as we do is the essential first step into adulthood, though it is astonishing how many supposed adults have never taken it.

I hasten to interject here, for those readers who worry that all of this encouragement of early maturity may result in the robbery of childhood, premature sophistication, or both, that what we would hope for is the development not of rigid, boring, or stodgy grown ups—tiresome people who take themselves far too seriously—but, rather, of adults motivated to make a positive difference in the world and to help others to do the same. The truly mature adult never loses touch with the inner child. Paradoxically, however, retaining the child*like* requires us to leave behind the child*ish*. The difference is easy to spot.

Recently my mother-in-law watched in astonishment as a "self-made" (that, of course, is a delusion in itself) multi-billionaire who owns a 43,000-square-foot vacation house furiously and wantonly destroyed the imaginary pirate ship a 4-year-old had built out of towels and wrought-iron cup holders on a beach adjacent to the sacred house, public property the wealthy man claims illegitimately as his. Why did he wreck the little boy's pirate ship? You'd have to ask the gentleman; apparently the child's fantasy offended his visual sensibilities. Clearly, the man's temporal power has deluded him to believe he can do as he wishes. Certainly this is not a man reconciled to his limits; and without question, he is either ignorant or terrified that, some fine day, his 43,000 square feet will be reduced to 12. The incident does lead one to wonder who is the 4-year-old here.

William Sloane Coffin, the wise former chaplain of Yale University, once said, "If you're disillusioned, remember you created the illusion in the first place."[9] A certain degree of disillusionment is necessary for us to accept ourselves for who we are—and the illusion of our immortality may be both the most difficult and the most important for us to shed. As long as we remain deluded that we are or should be all-powerful, we leave no room for anyone else. Not only do most of us occupy too much space now; most of us are working as hard as we can to take over ever more. The acceptance of our own limits means we no longer have to suck up all the oxygen in the room. Recognizing our limits opens our eyes to others struggling with theirs, and for the first time, relationship matters to us not just for the way it aggrandizes us but for what it does for both or even all of us. For us, then, identity and relationship are really one: embracing our mortality is, by definition, discovering we're not the center of the universe. Indeed, it is the merging of identity and relationship that signal's adulthood's arrival: it is the very nature of mature human beings to identify themselves in relationship.

With such a model of adulthood before them, emerging adults can take control of the pace and effectiveness with which they emerge, quite regardless of the availability of jobs, the mortgage rate, or their ability to find a soul mate. It is qualities like humility and care, integrity and self-possession, passion and compassion that identify us as adults, regardless of age and circumstance; indeed, they are the essence of true humanity. And isn't becoming fully human what adulthood is really about?

FCS

Brunswick, Maine
Spring, 2011

CHAPTER 1

Who's in Charge Here?

In the fifth grade, I had a classmate named Chuck Milland. I remember him as a nice kid, somewhat quiet, and, like the rest of us, pretty ordinary. And then one day something happened out of the blue that made him, at least in our eyes, extraordinary: Chuck's father committed suicide. And since he was a newspaper carrier for the Baltimore *Sun*—in fact, he happened to be my family's newspaper carrier—the event was reported on the front page in grueling detail.

When Chuck returned to school, he was no longer just another fifth-grader. We were quietly in awe of him. It wasn't the celebrity; it was that he'd crossed over into a universe about which most if not all of us were clueless. He seemed somehow years older. Like a battle-worn soldier who has visited the front, Chuck was suddenly a man experienced in the ways of life. Unfortunately, he no doubt interpreted the silent respect with which we responded to him as isolation and even rejection. I've always deeply regretted that—but who knows how to talk about such things in the fifth grade?

It's interesting to consider just what it was that, at least in our eyes, turned Chuck Milland into an overnight adult. It wasn't just his first-hand experience of death, though that was certainly part of it. Perhaps it occurred to us that now he had to become the dad; he had serious things to think about and do. 10-year-old Chuck would now suddenly have to play a more responsible role in his family. Our lives seemed somehow trivial when measured against his. Finally, of course, there was all of that grief, a complex of emotions that, we sensed, gave him a kind of emotional depth well beyond our understanding. And yet, as much respect as his new status garnered, it also drew our pity—Chuck's childhood had been cut short, and none of the rest of us, certainly, was ready to stop being a child.

Although few of us are thrust into adulthood at 10, of course, this story does serve to illuminate some of the qualities we often associate with maturity. But part of the trap into which my classmates and I fell as we observed Chuck from a distance was our focus on the seriousness of adulthood. I'm not sure we were quite cognizant of the fear and inadequacy Chuck must have felt, and certainly none of us talked to him about those things.

A different kind of brush with death by someone twice Chuck's age illustrates a contrary aspect of growing up—not growing into new authority and responsibility but outgrowing the illusion of power.

Years ago, when I was the Episcopal chaplain at Princeton, the son of a Princeton classmate of mine drowned when his car went into a canal not far from the University. I spent a good deal of time with the family and helped them prepare for the funeral, initially unaware I had another pastoral connection to the accident. But just a day or two later, I had a visit from a student who occasionally attended our services. As a volunteer EMT, he had been the first responder on the scene at the canal. The victim had still been alive inside the car struggling vainly to escape when the ambulance arrived. Because the water had disabled the car's electrical system, neither the doors nor the windows could be opened from inside or out. The EMT tried to break the windows, first with a branch and then with a signpost, but as the car was under water by that time, nothing worked. The image of a young rescue worker forced to stand by and watch, powerless to prevent the drowning of an equally young, strong, and uninjured victim, is acutely painful. I thought it might be mutually helpful for my young friend and the victim's parents to meet, and it surely was. But the newly forged friendship did little to assuage the pain and guilt.

And then it occurred to me that this young man was experiencing something neither friendship with the family nor counseling could touch—not just guilt but a kind of existential shame. His sin, if that's what it was, wasn't that he didn't do enough; he knew he'd done all he could. It was that all he could do still wasn't enough. And the only thing I could offer for that was absolution for the deficiency of being merely human.

The rarity of personal confession in the Episcopal Church is undoubtedly at least part of the source of its power. When I laid hands on my young friend and let him know that God loved him despite and maybe even because of his human frailty, I could sense the weight lifting. Though we shared silent tears, we said nothing at the time, eager not to disrupt the sense of transcendence. But a year later, he wrote to describe the moment in exactly the way I had experienced it. I wouldn't pretend to try to explain what took place that morning in the Princeton University Chapel; I simply rejoice in a young man's acceptance of his mortality and the new-found freedom that gave him.

What Chuck and the EMT each went through was akin to an earthquake—a sudden upheaval that altered their understanding of the universe. Someone I know who once lived through an earthquake told me the most terrifying thing about it was the sense that the Law of Gravity had been suspended, with no indication as it was happening of the duration of the suspension. Once you've been through an experience like that, how much confidence can you have going forward in the Law of Gravity?

The experiences of Chuck and the EMT, while obviously different in context, are both emblematic of the end of childhood. The illusion of every child that parents control everything disintegrated for Chuck with his father's suicide. The EMT had no doubt come to realize his parents weren't in charge; but his failure to save the drowning boy despite his very best efforts confronted him with the fact that he wasn't in control, either. So if no one else is in control, and we're not, either, then who is?

This is the theme of the biblical story of Job, which is based on an ancient Babylonian tale of a devoutly faithful man beset by misfortune who nevertheless retains his faith and is therefore rewarded with more than he lost, thereby demonstrating that good things happen to good people. Writing during the Babylonian Exile, which left the Israelites feeling betrayed by God and bewildered by what was going on, the Biblical author used the ancient and well-known story as the basis of his own expanded version to explore a more complicated insight: that sometimes, in fact, as best-selling author Rabbi Harold Kushner has famously observed,[10] bad things happen to good people.

In the biblical story, Job, a deeply faithful man who loses his fortune to fire, his children to natural disaster, and his health to the ravages of disease, finally doubts his faith. The question on his tongue is, "Why is this happening to me?" But the question in his heart is, "Is there anybody home up there? Or am I all alone? Who's running the show?" Job's friends, if you can call them that, trapped in the obsolete view that if you're faithful, you'll be rewarded, and that Job's doubt is the cause of his undoing, are the antithesis of compassion, upbraiding him for his faithlessness. Job dismisses them, knowing they don't know what they're talking about, and demands a face-to-face encounter with God, a demand with which God complies. While he doesn't even approach the question "Why?" and appears to do nothing but yell at Job, it is his *presence* that gives Job confidence that the responsibility for the universe hasn't come to rest solely on his own shoulders, and that he, Job, is not, finally, alone.

Like Chuck and the EMT, Job is not so much looking for someone to blame as he is searching for confirmation that *somebody* is in charge—that life is not simply random. Like Chuck, he knows any human agency on which he had previously depended is out of the loop on this one. And like the EMT, he is personally overwhelmed—his problems are clearly beyond his own agency.

How we answer the question, "Who's in charge?" has a lot to do with the kind of adults we become; *whether we even pursue it* determines whether or not we become adults at all.

Job and his friends had been chugging along quite nicely, assuming that the world worked according to a kind of retributive logic—good is rewarded, and evil isn't. Whether we're religious or not, many of us operate on that assumption, despite its obvious flaws. Certainly, it has never been true that bad things happen only to bad people. For some of us, it takes a tragedy to make us reflect on why things happen as they do; others have the foresight to consider that question in the abstract. At some point, though, our social, emotional and intellectual growth demands the conscious realization of the limits of our control.

Even as we acknowledge our limits, however, it is equally important to recognize the extent to which what we do matters. That we don't exercise ultimate control doesn't negate the far-reaching influence of the choices we do in fact make. Those who delude themselves into thinking they are fully in control are in danger of becoming narcissistic and dictatorial. Those who resist the idea that they have any control at all can fail to take responsibility even for their own lives let alone anyone else's. Even if you get the balance right, you are then faced with the question of what to do with the power you think you have.

If you've managed to avoid cataclysmic experiences like Chuck's and the EMT's, you have reason to be grateful. Yet surely both would affirm that mixed with the excruciating pain were unexpected and deeply significant insights that dawn on most of us with considerably more subtlety, if at all. While adolescence ought to be a time for coming to terms with these issues, for many, adolescence is either nothing more than extended childhood, in which one fails to realize the limits of other people's control, or half-baked adulthood, in which one fails to realize the limits of one's own control.

The testing of independence and exploration of autonomy that have traditionally been both the common fare of adolescents and the bane of their parents are unavoidable if one is to mature beyond adolescence. That testing is simply the manifestation of the question, "Who's in charge?" As wary as parents of teens are of that kind of testing, it's surely one of the signs that they're growing up. And the expectation is that, by their 20's, the testing period will be winding down and they'll begin to know how to be grownups. Today, that expectation is often unmet.

Branding an entire generation is both unfair and dangerous, but isn't it a fact that so-called "millennials" are beginning to be characterized as the generation that is declining to take charge? The *New York Times Magazine* asked pointedly in a feature article in August, 2010,[11] "Why are so many people in their 20's taking so long to grow up?" While the long article reaches an upbeat if somewhat labored conclusion—"if this longer road to adulthood really leads to more insight and better choices…an insightful, sensitive, thoughtful, content, well-honed, self-actualizing crop of grownups would indeed be something worth waiting for"—don't we still find ourselves asking, "Really? Until they're 35?"

All of that notwithstanding, there are plenty of millennials who don't fit the stereotype. In 1989, I was a cofounder of Princeton in Africa, an organization that develops year-long service fellowships for young college graduates in partnership with nonprofit organizations all over Africa. Our mission is to create a group of future Western leaders committed to Africa. Last year, we received 350 applications, a widely diverse pool geographically, economically, and ethnically, for 34 fellowships. Not one of those applicants is a stereotypical millennial. They are bright, talented, and highly motivated, and they know they can make a difference in the world with hard work and the right circumstances. They are full of initiative, passionate and focused, willing to take risks (all of them, after all, are seeking the road less traveled), ready to seize opportunity, and eager to use whatever power they have to spend the next year, at least, helping empower others. Interviewing and helping choose these fellows annually is both a difficult and inspiring privilege.

Clearly the altruistic energy of the Princeton in Africa applicant and the self-centered lethargy of the 22-year-old stuck in his parents' basement are at opposite extremes. But it may be worthwhile to look at why some end up at one extreme and some at the other. Both are subject to the same economic issues, the same wider culture. Yes, there may be something genetic going on. All Princeton in Africa applicants are bright, it's true—but there are plenty of very bright young people who seem disoriented or, at best, bemused by the world in which they find themselves, often vaguely ambitious but lacking in a sense of direction. What sets in for many is a kind of helplessness that terrifies them and disheartens their parents.

Can we identify the kinds of influences that produce young people ready to use the power they have in the service of others? And what's really going on in the life of the "stuck millennial"?

CHAPTER 2

Neither Here nor There

Josh Cooper will be 25 years old next month. A graduate of Hamilton College, he grew up in Westport, Connecticut, where he was a good student and athlete, though no star. (Lest Westport readers attempt to identify Josh, let me confess that he's entirely fictitious—but there are a lot of Josh Coopers out there.) His strong SAT scores and alumni-son status got him into Hamilton, where he was far more social than academic, with a GPA that meandered around 3.0. Unable to make varsity hockey or lacrosse, Josh dabbled in club sports. Though Hamilton offers a wide range of extra-curricular opportunities, Josh participated in only a few—notably his fraternity, where his outgoing personality and fun-loving spirit made him a natural for social chair.

Graduation from Hamilton left Josh a bit like Wylie Coyote, pushed off the cliff, flailing, with no forward motion. Like many in his class, he had sought out interviews in the financial world, though he wasn't quite sure why. The hedge fund managers and investment bankers with whom he spoke seemed surprised not just at his shallow knowledge of economics but also at his shallow reasons for wanting to work for them. (He tried to ice the cake as elegantly as he could, but it came down to money and status.) Josh received no callbacks—no surprise.

As Josh's parents had given him a trip to Europe as a graduation present, he was able to postpone the serious business of finding a job—but partying through Europe with classmates somehow failed to produce a revelation about what he should do with his life. Faced with the need for an income as his parents let him know living at home would require at least a modest financial contribution, Josh began to realize he might have to take a job unrelated to his future. To make matters worse, the economy had tanked, jobs were scarce, and many people like Josh were finding no opportunities at all.

Fortunately, Josh had social capital. His parents were well-connected, and he had access to the Hamilton College alumni network. A friend of his father's, coincidentally a Hamilton alumnus, ran a printing business in Stamford, less than 15 miles from Westport, and was looking for an executive assistant. The pay wasn't great, but health insurance was included, and though Josh was hesitant, his parents urged him to take the job.

"Executive assistant" turned out to be more of a "gofer" in a business that held little allure for Josh, but it was a job. Josh arrived home most nights demoralized by work that, while not overly taxing, did nothing to energize him. And while he got along well with his parents, the living situation could not help but increase the tension among them. With few friends in Fairfield County (What 20-somethings can afford to live in Fairfield County?), Josh spent as much time as possible with Hamilton friends in New York; but that solution had the downside of showing him the life he could have been leading.

Josh's New York buddies, largely banking interns and paralegals, seemed to be miles ahead of him vocationally, though, truth be known, not a few of them felt as lost and as infantilized as he did—they just looked more sophisticated, with their (closet-sized) New York apartments, the nightly bar scene, and the big paychecks (with no benefits and huge living expenses). They worked long hours doing grunt work, and while some were getting useful training, others bridled under their lowly status, of which they were regularly reminded by less-than-respectful supervisors. To be sure, some of Josh's friends were legitimately on their way to meaningful careers. But many were no better placed than Josh was in the printing business. It was a job and a paycheck, but it had little relation to who they were or wanted to be.

* * *

Untold numbers of people in their twenties seem stuck "in-between." Physically, at least, they're obviously no longer adolescents. But while the law recognizes them as adults, few of them readily identify themselves that way. [12] Too much in their lives conspires against their sense of independence, autonomy, and power. They lack status in their vocational lives, many resist or are unable to sustain a stable and committed relationship, they have no responsibility for anyone else, their social lives often retain a collegiate tone, and they are frequently somewhat rootless.

Developmental psychologist Jeffrey J. Arnett describes this group as "emerging adults" and believes that, as a group, they constitute a new stage of development—not simply a transition from adolescence to adulthood but a discrete stage unto itself. In *Emerging Adulthood*, he argues that the profound changes society has experienced in gender roles, reproductive control, the length and complexity of training required for participation in an information economy, and delayed marriage and parenthood have all contributed to the postponement of full-fledged adulthood in favor of a period of gradual maturation. [13]

Noting a similar phenomenon nearly half a century ago, Erik Erikson called it a "psycho-social moratorium." [14] But Arnett argues that what Erikson observed as "'prolonged adolescence" has become a different animal from adolescence altogether. [15] He notes a crisis of identity that is different in quality from that of adolescence—more serious, as the stakes are higher. Emerging adults, says Arnett, are more self-focused than at any other time in their lives; often still somewhat dependent on their parents though frequently groping toward a more equal relationship with them; and characteristically but paradoxically both optimistic and deeply anxious about the future. [16]

The problem with all of this is that it isn't universal. Lots of people either skip "emerging adulthood" or at least hurry through it, and many would argue that, far from being a stage of normal emotional growth, it is actually more suggestive of arrested development. Arnett himself admits that some people even in the industrialized world skip the stage, that it is rare in the developing world, and that, therefore, most people don't go through it at all. [17] As his good friend and fellow developmental psychologist Richard Lerner observes, "The core idea of classical stage theory is that all people — underscore 'all' — pass through a series of qualitatively different periods in an invariant and universal sequence in stages that can't be skipped or reordered." [18] In other words, if "emerging adulthood" is a stage, then it should happen to everyone. But clearly, it doesn't.

The argument is more than academic. If Emerging Adulthood is a legitimate stage of emotional development, then it will be important to give people the time and tools to move through it effectively. On the other hand, giving this period the status of a true "stage" may grant unwarranted permission for people to put off growing up.

In fact, I know another Josh—this one's real. He lives in Harpswell, Maine, is 19, and has been a lobsterman since he was 8. Josh just graduated from high school, and while he hopes to go to college, he believes he'll have to earn the tuition before he spends it. In fact, when and if he goes, he'll attend part-time so that he can continue his work as a lobsterman. Meanwhile, he's working fulltime, and having bought a small lobster boat last year and a new truck this year, he's saving for a down payment on a house. When Josh considers the future, he thinks about the possibility of fishing in Alaska, but chances are he'll be back in Maine plying the trade his family has been in for generations. At 19, Josh may not yet be an adult, but he's going to have to be one shortly. People like Josh Gatto don't have the time or the wherewithal for the luxury of "emerging adulthood."

So what's the difference between Josh Gatto and Josh Cooper? Josh Gatto learned when he was 10 that his parents couldn't afford the things many of his friends were getting from their parents—dirt bikes, computer games, and so on. Josh's parents told him if he wanted those things, he'd have to earn the money himself. That was Josh's first inkling that his parents didn't run the world. But unlike most 10-year-olds, Josh had a way to earn the money: he was already a licensed lobsterman. By the time he was 12, he had his own boat. He was given responsibility and readily took it on. Josh has had a chance to test his power in the real world, and while he's certainly aware of some of the limitations—he's had to work harder and play less than most of his peers—he has the breginnings of a self-possession that most of them still lack.

Josh Cooper, on the other hand, has experienced little that has encouraged him to take charge of his life, other than going away to school, a sheltered environment in which he certainly didn't push himself. He always knew he could fall back on his parents, an option not available to Josh Gatto. It may well be that expectations were never actually articulated in either family, but the difference is stark.

What's going to happen, then, to poor old Josh Cooper? Shall we simply leave him in this stage that may not even be a stage at all? The great thing about fictional characters is that the author controls their world, and this author is glad to report that Josh Cooper's story gets better—though not without some surprises and more than a little pain along the way.

* * *

A secretary at the printing plant mentioned to Josh that she was volunteering for a teen suicide prevention hotline. His interest in counseling having been piqued by a couple of psychology courses at Hamilton, Josh asked the secretary how he could get involved. As it happens, there was a training meeting that night, and he tagged along.

In short order, Josh went through the full training and became a regular, working at first one night a week and then asking for the chance to do more. He couldn't get enough of it; for the first time in his life, he felt he was doing something truly worthwhile. Most of the people who called in were just looking for attention, but he was glad to offer it. And on those occasions when there was a really serious emergency, he was able to garner the right combination of compassion, calm, and courage to talk the person through the moment. He wasn't sure where this was leading and didn't care; all he knew was that he felt good about what he was doing.

And then he got in over his head. The inevitable call came that he couldn't handle. Nothing he said seemed to matter. The teenager at the other end of the line was threatening to shoot himself, and Josh was powerless to stop him. To his horror, he heard an explosion and then silence.

Josh's mother found him early the next morning sitting on the back porch steps, gently weeping. She couldn't recall the last time she'd seen him cry. "Mom, he was just 17. And there was nothing I could do to stop him. I just can't get the sound of that gunshot out of my head."

Josh skipped work that day. But he didn't spend all day moping. He checked out counseling courses in the area and found he could enroll in one at the local community college that started the next month. Before long, he was taking two courses, still volunteering at the suicide prevention hotline, and, of course, working fulltime. The New York weekends went by the wayside, but he hardly noticed.

Then he caught a break. The assistant director of the agency running the hotline resigned because of a family move, and the director immediately offered Josh the job. The pay was paltry, the benefits thin, but he was finally able to dedicate all of his waking hours to what he cared about. And as his new boss was naturally supportive of his graduate work, Josh was able to arrange his time to take nearly a full load. He was well on his way to becoming an adolescent therapist.

Overnight, it seems, Josh Cooper grew up.

* * *

It wasn't the shot that grew him up; that only *woke* him up. Until the shot, nothing in Josh's life was compelling; he was rudderless. The illusion that all things were possible paralyzed him—he had no idea which way to turn, and it didn't seem to matter. His work for the suicide hotline gave him, for the first time, a sense of direction, a cause that fully engaged him. Until he began that work, Josh wondered how he could get the most out of whatever work he ended up in. Now what preoccupied him was how he could give more. He let go of his shallow dream of a life of luxury in favor of a life of meaning, drawn by his genuine and compassionate concern for the people on the other end of that phone line.

Perhaps it was the shot that finally forced Josh to ask, "Who's in charge here?" And the answer he came up with was, "I may not be able to solve every problem, but I can certainly do a lot more than I'm doing." But there's an interesting twist to Josh's answer to the question. After all, what he commits himself to is not just the increase of his own power but also the empowerment of others.

It's worth noting, as well, that Josh seized an opportunity. He took a chance when he attended that suicide prevention training. The world he entered was altogether different from the one in which he grew up or the one to which he had thought he aspired. He dared instead to follow his passion. Some equate adulthood with a kind of seriousness and stability that precludes both risk and passion. But people who are truly adult are willing to take reasonable chances and aren't afraid to care, because they've matured enough to know that all of life is a risk—indeed, one we'll lose in the end, in any case—and that to live without passion is to die before your time.

CHAPTER 3

Fear of Failure

If we think our parents are in charge, we spend our entire lives trying to please them. If we think we are, then we believe the entire universe depends on us. Either way, there's no room for failure—and that's tough, because all of us are destined to fail. But failure may turn out to be our greatest gift—not least because it helps explode all of those illusions.

That may sound like a strange way to talk about something most of us avoid at all cost, and for good reason. Hitting bottom, falling flat on your face, reaching the end of the line, coming up empty-handed—all are painful, humiliating experiences. In every case, something essential to who we are, or at least who we'd like to think we are, dies: a dream, an opportunity, a friendship, a romance, a job, status, security.

To make matters worse, most of us harbor a perfectionist streak, and more than a few of us are out-and-out perfectionists. The reason perfectionists demand flawlessness from themselves as well as others is that they don't believe they'll be loved for anything less. No matter how sure of themselves such people often seem, they feel as though they're always being judged and never quite measuring up. Of course, they are their own most exacting judges.

But it gets more complicated because while even perfectionists aren't perfect, there's no room in their universe to fail. Their only option, therefore, is to pretend they're someone they're not. On one level, then, they get through the day by convincing themselves they're pulling off this charade, but on a deeper level, they suspect, at least, that they're not getting away with it—and all the while, they know full well they're not being genuine. It's a tough way to live.

I speak from personal experience.

The first time I can remember becoming aware that I had a problem with perfectionism was my junior year of college, though I certainly must have had at least an inkling long before that. I had recently decided not to become a film score composer (having entered Princeton planning to be an architect), but for the first time in my young adult life, I hadn't the slightest idea what I wanted to do when I grew up. So I went to see the head of the Career Studies office, a clear-headed, thoughtful counselor named John McNaughton. It was the first time I could ever remember honestly seeking advice rather than trying to find someone who would tell me what I wanted to hear. I didn't know what I wanted to hear.

Mr. McNaughton listened patiently as I recounted my vocational hajj thus far, nodding a lot but saying little. When I assured him that I had decided against writing film scores not because I thought I couldn't do it but simply because I no longer wanted to—and even aggrandized that statement by adding that I had always assumed I could do anything I put my mind to—Mr. McNaughton took a long draught on his pipe, sat silently for a minute peering at me through a pair of piercing blue eyes, and finally asked, "Have you ever failed at anything?"

No one had ever asked me that question, and I was frankly stumped. I thought hard, and ridiculous as it seems to me now, I could think of nothing I'd failed at. I thought about the major goals I'd set for myself, and I'd met them all (or else, as I can see in hindsight, I'd reset them along the way in order to convince myself I'd met them all). And so, quite conscious that I was giving him the wrong answer but not knowing another to give, I responded (with an appropriate bit of hesitation, at least), "Um…no, I guess I haven't." "I think," said Mr. McNaughton, "that's your problem."

I left his office perplexed. Was I supposed to fail on purpose? Then I'd succeed at failing. That couldn't be the answer. Of course, I missed altogether the irony of what Mr. McNaughton *wasn't* saying: "You idiot! Of course you've failed. How can you be so dense? Or are you simply afraid to admit it?" All of the above. But difficult as it is now for me to believe, it took me several more years to figure it out, and even then I had to be conked on the head.

My vocational search took some surprising turns that spring and culminated in my discovery that I was going to be a teacher. It wasn't something I'd even thought about, really, but the more I imagined my future life in education, the more excited about it I became. I loaded up on American history courses and began applying to teach history. Ultimately, though, I was hired as an English teacher and dorm master at The Taft School, a boarding school in central Connecticut.

For the first time in my life, I threw myself into what I was doing 100%. Before that, I had always hedged, at least unconsciously, fearing that total commitment would expose me to the risk of failure which hedging enabled me to avoid by leaving me possible excuses for why things hadn't worked out. But at Taft, I couldn't hedge; quite simply, I cared too much. I was passionate about my students, and they knew it. I loved teaching even more than I'd imagined, despite my not having majored in English. Altogether, though I was flying by the seat of my pants, I was doing a decent job—and I'd never been happier. That my apartment was perpetually full of kids I took as confirmation that they loved me as much as I loved them. Life was good.

And then came Winter Term.

Winter Term at most New England schools is a time when people get edgy. Cold weather, gray skies, shorter days, and less outdoor time all tend to promote in the community a general irritability that was exacerbated at Taft, where much of the school was at that time under one roof. (Hockey is New England's principal cure for this malaise, but I didn't play.) Two weeks into Winter Term, I went to my mailbox, pulled out a letter with neither a stamp nor a return address, and began reading it as I climbed the stairs to my apartment.

The letter was unsigned but clearly from a student and ripped me limb from limb. "You think everybody loves you and that you're doing a great job. Well think again." That, at least, was the gist—and then the letter proceeded through the catalogue of my faults. Clearly, someone was incredibly angry at me—and, sad to say, incredibly perceptive. There were a few faults there that I honestly couldn't claim, but for the most part, he had nailed me.

I was devastated, though I can hear the reader responding, "It's just one kid." But that response misunderstands the perfectionist; one kid is one too many. Like Achilles, one chink in the armor, and I'm dead. And equally to the point, it's not just one kid. Because if perfectionists expend untold effort hiding from their vulnerability, they expend just as much magnifying it once it is irrevocably exposed. If one kid has found me out, how many others are there? Do they all know? The perfectionist lives in two realms—the delusion that he's getting away with the fraud of perfection he's perpetrating, and the terror that he could be found out at any moment.

That was my dilemma—only it was worse in this case. You see, this certainly wasn't the first time anyone had ever criticized me. But my strategy for dealing with criticism was to pre-empt. "You don't like me? Let me take you to lunch and convince you what a good guy I really am." Just how many people I fooled that way I'll never know; not many, I'm sure. But I had succeed more often than not in fooling myself.

This time, though, I was stymied. As I had no idea who the author was, I couldn't try to talk my way out of his anger. All I had was the letter, and I had no choice but to take what it said at face value.

And so I did. I read the accusations again and again and gradually, certainly not eagerly, but nevertheless willingly accepted what was true. It may have been the first completely honest moment in my life. And agonizing though it was, I remember thinking, "What an incredible profession this is, that you can feel so deeply about something like this." Perhaps not everyone would have. The reason I did is that I had committed myself so totally.

Strangely, however, I felt not despair but relief. Someone had just popped the balloon of perfection that I had spent most of my life keeping inflated. The balloon was destroyed, but I suddenly had a lot more breath. I realized I had always thought life was a straight line of progress on which people are meant to get better and better until they're perfect. It's a silly way to look at life, and yet I think if they're honest, most people look at it that way. Why else are we so afraid of failure? But it turns out progress isn't a straight line at all. It's a series of hills and valleys, and you can't get to the next hilltop without going through the valley. In fact, the height you are able to scale may be directly proportional to the depth to which you're willing to descend.

I'd like to be able to tell you that, as I left my apartment that evening, I was able to resist the temptation to look around and wonder, "Who wrote it? Was he the one? [Taft was at that time all-male.] Do they all know about it?" Of course that went through my head. But, fortunately, so did another thought which overtook the first. "Forget it, Frank. It doesn't matter. What matters is what's true. So take what's true, use it, and move on." And, remarkably, I did.

I don't know how many other people noticed the change in me, but I certainly did. I became more honest with myself and opened myself to more honesty from others. It's been a lifelong journey, of course, and I've done a lot of regressing. But that irretrievable failure stands out as one of the three or four most prominent landmarks on my spiritual journey, and I recognize it as the beginning of my adult life.

I have come to realize I am not the only person around who knows he's a fraud. Knowing you're not quite the person you present to others is part of being human—not the most attractive part, to be sure, but nonetheless endemic to human nature. Perhaps it's not a bad definition of sin, or at least, one aspect of sin. Knowing we're frauds can lead us in a variety of directions. We can waste a lot of energy maintaining the sham, as I spent the first 20-odd years of my life doing, though generally we're not as good at the subterfuge as we think. We can try to minimize the deception by avoiding those circumstances that are likely to expose us. I play the piano, and honesty, not false modesty, forces me to admit that people think I'm a lot better than I am, a result both of my ability to fake a lot and of most people's lack of discrimination about such things. I find myself so disconcerted by the inconsistency that I just don't play much anymore, except occasionally when no one else is listening.

Finally, we can throw in the towel and confess the fraud. But that route can be disastrous. Because if you come to the conclusion that you're *nothing* but a fraud, and there is no one around to help you see otherwise, what's left? Not infrequently, people commit suicide when everyone else thought they were at the top of their game. In fact, they were; they just didn't see anywhere to go from there but down.

The issue here is what finally scares us most about failure: that, in the end, we'll be left all alone. And that, of course, is why failure, loss, and death are all really about the same thing—because they all seem to result in our complete isolation. But is that necessarily the case?

There is one more option for dealing with our fraudulence that suggests not. We can confess it to someone who cares about us, although, because our dishonesty has betrayed them, doing so risks their legitimate betrayal of us. Nevertheless, despite the risk and perhaps because of it, confessing to someone who cares is doubly valuable: first, it's the most honest approach, since you're allowing yourself to be accountable not just to yourself but to someone else, as well; and second, you're giving someone a chance to forgive you. That forgiveness is what will let you know not only that you are a great deal more than just a fraud but also—and most important— that you are not alone.

Forgiveness has a good many definitions, but the most helpful one here is the promise to continue to care despite the past. All of us fear that, at some level, we are too guilty to be forgiven. We live, therefore, with the terror that, when our guilt comes to light, everyone will reject us. And yet the very act of confessing that guilt to someone who loves us almost always has the effect of increasing their love, because more powerful than the sin of which we're guilty is the vulnerability with which we confess it, which enables the vulnerability of others. For better or worse, it's very hard to believe in the efficacy of placing ourselves at such risk until we actually dare to do it.

But how do we find the courage to face failure? Sometimes, of course, it's not a choice. Circumstances—like some anonymous person placing a poison-pen letter in your mailbox—may virtually force you to face it, though, to be sure, I could have responded to that situation with a large dose of denial and continued the pretense. Of course, I would have been the loser. While what happens to us is frequently beyond our control, we generally have a choice about how we react to it.

How, then, can we build up our nerve, so that the fear of failure stops undermining us? The simple answer is the same as the one in that tired old vaudeville joke about how to get to Carnegie Hall: practice. The experience of embracing failure and discovering, in the process, that you don't die of it is the only way to become sufficiently confident to make that a regular habit. Unfortunately, it's not a lesson you learn once and for all; you have to keep re-learning it, because the fear of failure has a nasty way of sneaking up on you, especially when you think you have it licked. That's our lot as human beings.

Living with the fear of failure is a lot like living with impending death, of which cancer surgeon Bernie Siegel has written poignantly in *Love, Medicine, and Miracles*.[19] Dr. Siegel noticed that when he told his patients when they were going to die, they usually did so right on cue. But realizing that his predictions were based purely on statistical averages and that human beings aren't statistics, he began fudging his predictions and giving his patients more hope. To his astonishment, they almost always lived longer. This observation led him to transform his patient care as he became far more sensitive to some of the nuances of the dying process. Siegel came to understand that patients suffering from terminal illness have a choice. They can spend their last days, weeks, and years consumed by their illness, in essence dying before their time. Or they can choose to live until they die.

Like the fear of death, fear of failure keeps us from being fully ourselves. We spend our lives second-guessing ourselves, hedging our bets in order to make sure we don't lose. The problem is that no one wins all the time; ultimately, we're all losers. But we can choose to live until we lose, refusing to be consumed by who and what we're not, taking the risk of being who we are—because to try to be anything else is actually far riskier.

It's all, finally, about letting go of control—but we can make that easier on ourselves by facing the fact that we're letting go of control we never had in the first place. Once again, the question is, "Who's in charge here?" And while the answer seems unequivocal—"Not I"—it turns out that honesty with ourselves gives us more control than we ever realized we had.

It's not just a matter of embracing each failure as it comes along, then. What we're all called to do, finally, is accept ourselves, limited, bumbling, mortal souls that we are. Is there a better definition of growing up?

Chapter 4

Identity and Relationship

He fell in love with her on a Metro North commuter train. Sitting by the window next to an empty seat engrossed in a counseling textbook, he was suddenly distracted by an enchanting voice that seemed simultaneously to sing and speak. Looking up from his book and observing first the speaker and then her seat mate, he thought, "She doesn't belong with that guy;" something about the pair's interaction didn't seem right. And then as he continued to eavesdrop, it became apparent that the guy, not the girl, was the one trying with only limited success to make conversation.

Josh called to her across the aisle, "Forgive me—I couldn't help overhearing your conversation. Did you say you went to Stanford?" To the deep chagrin of her erstwhile companion, Melanie immediately got up and sat in the empty seat next to Josh, replying with gratifying enthusiasm that betrayed both interest and relief, "Yes, I did. Why do you ask?" "It's silly, really," said Josh. "Stanford is a big place. But my best friend from high school went there and I thought you might know him." Then, lowering his voice and glancing briefly at the fellow across the aisle, he added, "And it looked to me like you could use a little help."

And so it began. They were both headed to New York—Josh to his counseling program at NYU, Melanie to Columbia Teachers College, where she was pursuing a master's degree. As she got off at 125th St., they agreed to meet for dinner that night. Then it was lunch the next day, dinner and jazz Saturday night, dinner every night the following week, a weekend with friends on a boat in Long Island Sound, and in no time, they were inseparable. It was like an endless honeymoon with someone you felt you'd known all your life. Before the month was out, they began to talk about moving in together, both eager at last to stop living with their parents and just as eager to spend as much of their lives together as possible. Melanie got word of a West Side studio apartment that, between Josh's modest income and Melanie's savings from her two years of teaching, they could barely manage, and Connecticut became history.

So, unfortunately, did the honeymoon. As they settled into ordinary life, little things began to gnaw at each of them. Melanie had an annoying habit of setting the alarm an hour early so that she could have the pleasure of turning it off and staying in bed another hour. But the same alarm would leave Josh, always a light sleeper, wide-awake and unable to get back to sleep. She took endless showers. She talked endlessly on the phone. Josh left his clothes on the floor wherever he happened to take them off, failed to use coasters for glasses on coffee tables, and apparently thought the dishes in the sink would ultimately wash themselves. She was a neatnik; he was a slob. She was Ms. Organization; he was Mr. Spontaneous. She nagged; he moped. They spent an increasing amount of their time together arguing—about their plans, about the apartment, about their assorted habits, about the weather. In one especially explosive moment, Josh complained, "I don't need you to be my mother," to which Melanie retorted, in a voice that neither sang nor spoke but seethed, "Well I sure don't need you to be my child." The apartment was small—*very* small—and these two who had been so eager to spend every waking moment together were now desperate to get away from each other.

Before long, they were scheduling meetings at night and on the weekends and digging up any excuse they could find to be apart, until at last, Melanie said to Josh, "We need to talk."

* * *

Relationships are what make us human, but they are unendingly complicated. Surely one of the most challenging things about them is that they don't really begin as relationships at all, though that's what they look like.

When Josh first heard and then saw Melanie, he certainly thought what he was doing was relating to another person. And objectively, he was. But consider that, of the hundreds of women he had seen that morning, Melanie was the only one who stopped him in his tracks, though all he did was hear a few words and see what she looked like. How, on such slim evidence, could Josh have known that Melanie was someone he'd like to get to know well, let alone enough to get his heart racing?

We make such judgments all the time, of course. You're sitting in a busy airport, absently people-watching. "He looks like a nice guy." "Wouldn't want to get caught in a dark alley with him." "What an adorable little girl." "She clearly thinks highly of herself." Not one of these people has spoken. All of your opinions are based on fleeting glances, yet you construct whole narratives around those snapshots.

In such brief encounters, we're not really relating to other people. What we're relating to is our projections onto those people. Why don't you want to get caught in a dark alley with that guy? Perhaps because he looks like someone you remember, or because he awakens a primal fear with the angry expression on his face. But maybe he's had a stroke, and his face is frozen into that expression. He may not be angry at all and would surely pose no threat in an alley, dark or otherwise.

Similarly, Josh and Melanie know virtually nothing about each other and base a great deal on their projected assumptions. The reason Melanie gratefully moves over to sit with Josh is that, while she doesn't know he went to Hamilton, she can tell nevertheless from his clothes and general bearing that he and she likely share a good deal, just as she has determined pretty quickly that she and her former seat mate have little in common. She may well know Josh's high school friend, and if not, then there are likely no more than 2 degrees of separation.

Well, that's a start. That they both have attended highly selective colleges, however, doesn't necessarily make them a natural couple. Josh and Melanie are each drawing from deep within themselves—their memories, their histories, their families, their friends, their whole worlds—to keep this relationship going, at least as deeply from within themselves as from each other. Since they don't know each other well yet, they fill in what they don't know with their own material, and clearly, they are both excited about what they have created. What they are entirely unprepared for, however, is that the person each of them has created turns out not to be the person each of them ends up living with.

Josh and Melanie are at one of the essential turning points of the growing-up process—one some people never get past. If growing up is, in part, discovering who you are, it is also about the discovery that you can't be fully you all by yourself. John Donne wrote, "No man is an island, entire of itself." The 20's can be an especially self-focused time when the search for vocation becomes all absorbing. Making choices that may well have life-long consequences, as one often must do in one's 20's, can be sufficiently daunting that everything else, including the other people in one's life, seems trivial by comparison, encouraging a degree of self-centeredness that is certainly not conducive to relationship-building. And yet this is also the very time for many when our ability to form meaningful and lasting relationships is tested. People like Josh and Melanie, then, find themselves drawn into a relationship at the very same time that they are feeling especially protective of their personal prerogatives.

We all know people who have tried to resolve this crisis by putting either their relational or their vocational lives on hold. What makes that solution less than optimal for most people is that both our vocational and our relational needs are beckoning at the same time, and to live into our full identities—i.e., to grow up—we need to respond in both directions at once, though relationship and vocation don't always work in tandem. Indeed, learning to recognize and work out the conflicts is one of the tasks of maturity.

Relating genuinely to an *other* may be the greatest challenge we face in our lives. Most of us grow up relating to parents and siblings—people who are, for all intents and purposes, stuck with us, and with whom we're stuck, to cast the situation in its worst light. But building a love relationship with a partner is to relate to someone whom we have chosen and who has chosen us. That the same is true, for the most part, of friends as we grow up is the reason friends float in and out of our lives. Making the intentional decision to love another human being is perhaps the most completely mature action any of us ever takes. And make no mistake—love is an intentional decision. Lust we have little choice about; our attractions work beyond our control. But love is not a feeling; it is the decision to care about another regardless of how you feel at the moment. Love is unconditional—and while it is always a leap of faith, it is a leap we make with our eyes wide open. Anything else would not be a choice made freely, and mature choice is the essence of love. At the same time, it is the very act of loving another human being that draws us out of ourselves, frees us from our self-absorption, and imbues us with a new and refreshing magnanimity. That's the ideal—and it isn't easy to come by.

For Josh and Melanie, that magnanimity is elusive. As deeply as they are digging into their careers at this point, they've only scratched the surface with each other. Once they have to live with each other, they begin to discover the hard work and costly investment a deep relationship requires. All of us are subject to contradictory motives when it comes to bonding with other people. The egocentricity with which our lives begin and even continue forces our psyches to trick us into relationship with others. Hence, all "relationships" begin as something far more internal than we realize. We may be talking, working, and living with what appears to be someone else, but what we're relating to is not really another person at all but an individual we've constructed in that person's place. That's why most married people report the experience, sometimes even during the honeymoon, of having looked at their spouses and thought, "Who is this person I married?" Over time, we finally withdraw our projections and actually relate to the other human being as other, though in the course of the relationship, we inevitably revert to projections that cloud our view of the real person with whom we're relating.

Relating to others, then, is a dynamic process that begins internally but gradually pulls us out of ourselves. It's one of the true miracles of being human. After all, we could just as well have been created as completely independent automatons that, at best, simply bounced off of one another rather than reaching into one another. Instead, we are not only attracted to others but also enriched by them—ultimately, our very identities are expanded by our relationships. But all of that doesn't usually happen in an instant. Most of us crawl out of our shells at best reluctantly, and even when we dare to venture out, we're ready to crawl back in at the first sign of something unexpected.

Josh and Melanie have barely begun to relate to one another as the people they really are; instead, each is infatuated by an imaginary person, and when occasionally the real person breaks through, the effect is so jarring that it scares them back into their separate corners. Objectively speaking, one could make a case that Melanie is playing the role of the mom and Josh, that of the child. But those roles are encouraged by each of their projections. Melanie's tone when Josh leaves his clothes on the floor floods Josh with memories of his mother scolding him for the same thing. And Melanie, in turn, hears herself becoming her mother, treating Josh as her mother had treated her, or perhaps as her mother had treated *her* father. But Melanie isn't a mom, and Josh isn't a child; they are simply drawing out those behaviors in each another. The problem in all of this is that the real people in the drama have completely disappeared, and projections are all that's left. Without real people, relationships fall apart.

It's reasonable to imagine that Melanie's follow-up to "We need to talk" is "I'm out of here." But suppose that isn't what she says at all?

Suppose, instead, Melanie says to Josh, "We need to talk—because something happened today that turned my world upside down, and I need you."

* * *

And then Melanie told Josh of the call she'd received from the mother of one of her old 7th grade students telling her that the girl had been shot the day before, the innocent victim of a gang fight, and had died instantly. The victim, now 15, had been one of her favorite students, and Melanie remained close to both the girl and her family.

Even as Josh held Melanie, trying to comfort her, he could hear the gunshot that still echoed from that failed crisis-line call several years ago, and he was stricken with grief for his own loss, which he found himself reliving in every detail, as well as Melanie's. All of the petty battles of the past few months disappeared in that moment, replaced by matters of life and death. And the petty battles weren't all that was replaced. The event shocked Melanie and Josh into reality, and her vulnerability in asking for his help elicited his vulnerability in giving it. If it is our defensiveness that is largely responsible for our projections, then nothing dissolves those projections faster than willing vulnerability.

When Melanie told Josh she needed to go immediately to the girl's home to visit with her parents and teenage siblings, he asked if she'd like him to join her, since perhaps his professional skills might be useful. She was grateful not to have to make the condolence call alone, and the sharing of this event became the bond that rebuilt their relationship. Josh had told her earlier about the suicide call and, in the next couple of days, poured out his own stored grief in a way that let Melanie know he understood some of what she was feeling.

What happened to Melanie and Josh is that, for the first time, they truly *cared* for each other, in both senses of the word—i.e., had tender feelings for each other, and took responsibility for each other. What had been going on until then was a parallel affiliation in which, like swimmers about to enter cold water, they waded in gradually, all the while asking themselves, "Am I enjoying this?" Nearly absent was any depth of responsibility for the other. In fact, there really was no other, because they were relating largely to creations of their own psyches.

Now that a real other person inhabited each of their lives, they were jolted into caring for each other. Paradoxically, it was Melanie's immediate need for emotional support that made her sensitive to Josh's own need. It doesn't always work that way. The tragically high divorce rate among parents who lose a child suggests that the simultaneous neediness of both members of a couple can place a marriage at risk. Neediness can so smother our customary inner resources as to leave us feeling inadequate to take care of anyone.

But having already begun to grapple with the pain of his mortality and come to terms with it, Josh was able to respond as an adult to Melanie. Rather than frightening him into paralysis, as it might well have done to someone less experienced with violent death, the event drew out Josh's empathy, enabling him to reach out to Melanie in a mature, compassionate way that empowered her own maturity and compassion.

Though Josh will never completely rid himself of the ache of that suicide, what he did manage to do in its aftermath was to wrestle his fear and guilt to the ground. Those existential responses to death—the fear of loneliness and the guilt and fear associated with our powerlessness— are what confound us until we finally refuse to let them control us. Josh learned to live with his mortality and the limits on his power imposed by his humanity, and though life for him has been admittedly more painful, it has also been made far more vital by his newfound depth. Of course, even he forgot much of that in the midst of his quotidian domestic issues with Melanie—these are not lessons we learn just once—but now that Melanie was involved in the same struggle, what they shared was becoming precious and lasting.

* * *

Theologian Martin Buber identified two polar opposite relationships in human experience: I-It, and I-you.[20] In the I-It relationship, I treat the other as an object to whom I relate only for my own benefit. I am so oblivious of others that I assume everything and everyone revolves around me. I don't even really acknowledge the otherness of the person to whom I'm relating, for as far as I'm concerned, that person is relevant only insofar as he or she has to do with me.

A surprising number of our relationships never get beyond I-it. That's especially true of people with whom we always engage in the same way—the clerk at the pharmacy, the mail deliverer, the airline ticket agent—people who serve us briefly and about whom we either make a host of assumptions on the basis of extremely limited information or else largely ignore. If we actually take time to relate to such people as people and discover they're also husbands or wives, parents, jazz-lovers, or tennis-players, we can get beyond the two-dimensionality of an I-it relationship. Friends are often surprised that some of my best book recommendations come from the man who mows our lawn.

Tragically, I-it relationships aren't confined to people we barely know. We are perfectly capable, as Melanie and Josh demonstrate, of treating those we know as objects. Because such habits run deep, being intentional about recognizing the humanity in those close to us can be as challenging as making that effort for those we simply meet in passing.

The I-you relationship, by contrast, is completely giving and demands nothing. I love for the sake of loving and out of the conviction that you are worthy of my love without regard to your willingness to love me. Of course, the real miracle occurs when I and you give ourselves completely to each other—a miracle because I have done nothing to compel you, and you have done nothing to compel me. It is love freely given, and given with no demand for anything in return; the relationship's mutuality is a gift for both me and you. I include you and you include me, though I am not all of who you are, and you are not all of who I am. A perfect representation of this notion is the "yin" and "yang" of the Tao, Lao-Tzu's paradoxically balanced image both of the origin of all things and of the "Way of Life." I have often observed that marriage is not a state in which husband and wife are meant to become identical, nor, certainly, is one meant to control the other. Rather, even as the two become one, they do so in a way that preserves the personhood of each, so that the empowerment of each results in the empowerment of both.

But if you're still fighting the battle of "Who's in charge here?" and scratching out your little patch of control, it's probably difficult to imagine that the most powerful way for you to use that control is to yield it to someone else. That involves a huge risk—letting a piece of yourself die, the self that is so preoccupied with "me" that there isn't much room for anyone else, the self that is so busy demanding control as to have failed as yet either to discover or to accept how little it has. In the I-You relationship, I give myself up completely to you. And the reason that gift ultimately empowers me is that what I give up of myself turns out to be expendable, because what is left is me, reborn.

Look at Josh and Melanie. No longer confined by the fear that one would control the other, each is now freed by the willingness to give up control, with the result that, simultaneously, both are in control, and neither is in control. Though each of them had been hanging onto their old selves for dear life, those selves were taking a severe toll on each of them and destroying who they were together. Letting go, they enabled a new sense of themselves independently and, at the same time, the creation of a new being, Josh-and-Melanie.

Erik Erikson characterized adolescence and young adulthood as a period of identity quest, but he might just as well have focused on the quest for relationship, for precisely what we discover as we mature is that identity and relationship are inextricable. None of us is as discretely and monolithically individual as we think we are. Commonly, we understand the "self" to be "an individual." Nothing frames this definition better than Descartes' well-known dictum, *Cogito, ergo sum*: I think, therefore I am. Thinking is—usually, at least—a solo exercise, and Descartes clearly has in mind a lone individual. I would suggest, however, that it is the nature of human beings not to be alone but rather, to be existentially connected to others. "I relate, therefore I am." From the very moment the umbilical cord is cut, the illusion of our independence begins; but while we are no longer physically attached to anyone, we are nevertheless bound to others by our manifest inability to take care of ourselves entirely independently.

From earliest childhood, though being physically distinct from others may mislead us into imagining ourselves in isolation, who we are is substantially determined by our relationships—to our parents, our siblings, our mentors, our friends, our enemies, our lovers, our spouses, our children, and the countless people in our lives whose classification is amorphous. Our identities include everyone we've ever met and, indeed, many we haven't—our great-great grandmothers; our great-great grandchildren; people on the other side of the globe of whose relation to us we may be entirely unconscious. They are all part of who we are. Not that we are *only* the sum of all of those people. But whatever about us is unique is so bound up with all of those relationships that it is undiscoverable in isolation. And even if we could discover it, it would be neither the whole of who we are nor even the kernel. Even our genetic makeup—perhaps the most personal thing about us—is determined by relationship. There is only one *you* in the world. There has only ever been one *you*, and there will never be another. But the *you* that is so completely unique isn't a solo act. It's an entanglement of human interactions, of physical contact, of psychic engagement, of the converse of ideas, of the traffic jams of emotions that constitute human relationship.

From the very first, then, we've been about relationships. What changes dramatically as we grow up is the nature of those relationships. As children, we perceive all relationships in terms of ourselves. Growing up is realizing that others are at least as important as we are and that relationship is not just about preserving me but at least equally and perhaps substantially more about caring for you. To relate maturely is to understand the other as both entirely separate from you and completely deserving of your concern and engagement by the simple virtue of being another human being.

* * *

The reader will surely not be surprised that, after two years together, during which Josh and Melanie helped each other to grow up, he at last asked her to marry him, though by this time, the marriage was a foregone conclusion not only to them but to virtually everyone who knew them. By then, they'd seen each other's best and worst, and even without the formal promises, each knew the other would be there no matter what. They'd lived through the initial excitement, the subsequent disillusionment, and the rediscovery of each other that came once they were willing to accept and value each other not for the person each might have liked the other to be but *as is*. Will marriage end their petty fights? No—but what arguments they have will seem trivial and short-lived in the context of their mutual realization that what they have together isn't just the exuberant feelings that initially attracted them to each other but something much deeper—the *decision* each has made to love the other without condition. Their vows bespeak not simply their emotional attachment to each other but something more grounded: "for better for worse, for richer for poorer, in sickness and in health, to love and to cherish, until we are parted by death."

As each has grown into an acceptance of the other as *another*, both Melanie and Josh are now ready to make such vows. And as they do so, they will begin to revel in the adventure of continuous discovery not only of that other person but of themselves, as well—for Melanie and Josh will never again be the same people they are the day they marry. Because people have the capacity to grow and change throughout their lives, they will no doubt sometimes mystify, annoy, and even infuriate each other. Their romantic ardor will ebb and flow. They will continue to be independent people, each with his or her own set of values, views, quirks, and so on. But they will also influence each other, so that Melanie, without really intending to do so, will begin to draw out Josh's unconscious need for order, just as she will begin to reflect Josh's spontaneity. It isn't that they will absorb each other—their personalities are both too strong for that to happen—but each will help the other to become a whole person, exposing aspects of their personalities formerly hidden and unexplored.

Before long, they'll have children, and their vows to each other will now extend to include these new beings who so depend on them. Being needed can feel like a trap, but the freedom each will have already discovered in loving the other will grow into a new sense of vitality and meaning in the infinite love and care of their now-extended family. Will they likely hit some bumps in the road? Of course. They're bound to encounter financial strains, illness, death, cranky teenagers, a learning disability or two, a leaky roof here or there, and sundry other problems, both solvable and unsolvable, not to mention issues between the two of them over their ever-changing relationship with each other and the rest of their family. But they'll be pretty well prepared to deal with whatever comes their way, because these are two *adults* who, with the help of their mature resources, will have built a healthy marriage and family. Whatever they face, they'll face together with their independent and mutual intelligence, passion, energy, and integrity. They'll share adventures and quiet moments, mutual presence and memories in common. As they grow old together, they will often seem as one—Melanie-and-Josh—even as they continue to encourage each other's growth into the individuals each would never have become without the other. Along with their children and grandchildren, there will be no one for whom each of them cares more than the other, and their trust will be complete.

If this marriage sounds idyllic, it is nevertheless the predictable fruit of the mature commitment of Josh and Melanie to each other. The idea that marriage is itself evidence of maturity is belied both by our society's high divorce rate and by the less-than-mature behavior husbands and wives not infrequently inflict on each other. People don't suddenly become adults because they get married, and while the marriage of people who are not yet adults may not be doomed, its survival is certainly in doubt. The prospects are good for the marriage of Melanie and Josh in no small part because they are adults. To be sure, if the marriage works, it will encourage their continued maturity, but their adulthood will be marked by the result not of the fact of their marriage but of all of the strength of character and love they both bring to it.

CHAPTER 5

Empathy, or Getting Over the Fairness Doctrine

Every Thursday evening, I attend meetings of Rebound, a program for troubled teens. Most are referred by the courts in lieu of conviction and sentencing in favor of a friendlier form of rehabilitation. Twice during my tenure as a mentor, we've talked in the group about fighting. Now, most if not all of the mentors are reasonably well attuned to teenagers and care deeply about them; they wouldn't be involved in this program if they weren't. And most of the teenagers seem to genuinely like most of the adults and appreciate our being there, as they know we're there for them. But each time the subject of fighting came up, the adults and teens found themselves, uncomfortably, in separate universes.

During the second of these discussions, we focused, with her willing permission, on a girl I will call Anita. She had made her way to Rebound courtesy of a fight with another girl who had pressed charges against her. As she recounted the history of her relationship with the other girl, you could watch the adults become more and more incredulous. "We've had three major fights. The first was in middle school," Anita began. "She was just constantly annoying me, so finally I hit her. She was a lot smaller than I was—in fact, she still is." Then she added with obvious pride, "I really clobbered her." While the adults groped for an appropriate response, Anita continued. "In 9th grade, she challenged me to a fight. I don't know why—she must have known I'd clobber her again. And I did. So this year, she started running her mouth on the Internet about me, and I had just had it. I let her know I was going to beat her up. Other kids from school heard about it, so we had quite a crowd egging us on. She started mouthing off again, and I slugged her in the eye. You could hear her cheekbone crack when I did it." She said this last sentence with some satisfaction, though there was perhaps just a hint of regret. It was frankly hard to tell. Finally, one of the mentors spoke up. "So what did that prove?" "That she shouldn't go running her mouth on the internet about me," replied Anita a bit defensively, and other teens in the room chimed in with nods or "Yeah's." "So what if you'd had a gun," asked another mentor. "Would you have shot her?" Anita replied, "I don't know. Maybe." At that point, one of the other kids shouted, "She deserved it!" and most of the other young people nodded in agreement.

I asked Anita, "Do you respect this girl?" to which she replied, "No, not at all." "Do other people respect her?" "Absolutely not," said Anita, and a few others corroborated that judgment. "So why," I asked, "do you care so much what she says?" As Anita stared at me, thinking about my question, I went on, "You could have simply turned on your heel and ignored her. Instead, she got exactly the rise out of you she was hoping for, and you gave her all the power." Seeing the quizzical look on her face, I went on, "After all, she may have lost the fight, but you're the one sitting here in Rebound for 11 weeks, right?"

But once again, another teen said, "But that girl deserved what she got," and there appeared to be among the young people in the room a consensus that the fight was therefore justified. "I couldn't just walk away," added Anita. At that point, one of the mentors broke in to say that while her older child had gone to high school in a neighboring town, her younger one had attended the high school most of these young people attend now. While there was virtually no fighting at all at her older child's school, she observed that there seemed to be a "culture of fighting" at our local high school, and that, therefore, walking away wouldn't have been easy. To walk away from a fight would mean losing face, a breech of the school culture's definition of honor. That helped to explain why all of these kids were of one mind on this issue.

I tried one more argument. "Suppose this girl had been 8 years old and had been disparaging you on the Internet. Would you have hit her then?" "Of course not," Anita quickly answered. "Why not?" I asked. "Because she's only 8." "But you've said you have no respect for the girl you hit. She's acting like she's 8. Why not treat her that way?" I think, perhaps, that made her think; she didn't have an immediate response. But I'm pretty sure neither she nor any of her peers changed their minds. We reached the end of our time together with no real resolution, and the adults left feeling as though we were up against a brick wall.

It has since occurred to me that the reason for the great divide between the older and younger people in the room is that all of the younger people are still wedded to the Fairness Doctrine. The Fairness Doctrine, which I formulated early in my role as a parent, states quite simply: *Everything must be fair*. The Fairness Doctrine is, as every parent knows, one of childhood's central tenets, and is the battle cry of virtually every child in negotiations with parents. The Fairness Doctrine, however, is accompanied by The Fairness Corollary, which always takes children by surprise: *Nothing is ever completely fair*. No matter how hard you try, someone is going to think he's getting ripped off, because the assessment of fairness is entirely dependent on the point at which you start to measure it as well as the point of view of the measurer.

As a small child, I spent a good many afternoons with a little girl from up the street. She was a year younger than I and the only other child close to my age in the neighborhood. I can remember the two of us sitting in my family's den having Cokes. I would down my Coke in a single gulp while she sipped daintily. Then I'd point out that she had nearly a whole glass, while mine was empty—clearly unfair—and I'd take her glass and poor half of it into mine. Then I'd drink that and do it again. I guess she didn't care much about the Coke, because she let me get away with that nonsense repeatedly. Clearly, I had the makings of a little dictator; fortunately, I never found any other willing subjects.

The obsession with fairness and a sense of entitlement seem to feed each other. While we're quick to consider what we deserve, we rarely take account of what we have that we *don't* deserve; we leap instead to what we don't have that we think we do deserve. I did nothing to deserve my first breath, yet here I am. In fact, when I stop to think about the things that matter most about me, I realize I did nothing to deserve any of it. Likewise, when I consider people who, through no fault of their own, suffer terrible misfortune, "deserving" seems to have nothing to do with it.

If a wealthy man inherits a million dollars and a starving homeless person takes ten dollars from him, the wealthy man is likely to cry, "Unfair! You did nothing to deserve that ten dollars; it's mine." Of course, the wealthy man has done nothing to deserve to be a millionaire, either, but he's conveniently forgotten that. And it may well be that the homeless person has done nothing to deserve his hunger and homelessness—we don't know that story. Fairness is all in who's doing the measuring.

Another problem with the Fairness Doctrine is our tendency to use it to justify almost any behavior. Anita admitted she might have used a gun if she'd had one. What makes that believable is that so many young people all over the country die of gunshot wounds. Murder is second only to unintentional injury as a cause of death among 15-to-19-year-olds in America.[21] Anita is clearly not alone. Throughout the conversation at Rebound I kept hearing in my mind my wife's admonition whenever any of our kids got physical: "Use your words." Here we have high school teenagers breaking kindergarten playground rules. No one has taught them to use their words. And their defense is the same one my children used to give, "But it wasn't fair," as though the unfairness didn't simply justify the fight—it made it both inevitable and necessary. One girl said she actually enjoyed fighting, and since she is, in other circumstances, a thoroughly kind and respectful young woman, I suspect what she enjoys is the sense that she's righted a wrong—that the Fairness Doctrine has been reinstated. Not that fairness is in itself wrong—it is simply not enough. The young people in Rebound treated fairness as though it were the only principle that matters.

Fairness isn't, however, the best we can do. It is the minimum standard for human behavior, given our propensity for greed, selfishness, and overreaction. Hammurabi's Code invoked "an eye for an eye" because, formerly, it had been customary to demand a life for an eye. It doesn't require genius, though, to realize that the literally retributive justice of an eye for an eye leaves two people blind and fails to solve any problems beyond simple revenge. But it *is* fair.

Precise fairness, more often than not, is a futile goal. Is it fair that students with learning disabilities get more time on tests than those without? Would it be fair for such students not to get extra time? Literal fairness—i.e., everyone being treated exactly alike—is nonsensical in such a situation. What is possible is to try to provide for everyone's needs. If everyone gets what he needs, everyone should be satisfied. But make no mistake—this is not the Fairness Doctrine.

Moreover and probably most important, while the Fairness Doctrine may be enshrined in childhood imagination, it isn't one of the immutable laws of the universe; in fact, the way of the world, on close examination, is manifestly *unfair*. That's what Job discovers, though his friends remain in denial. Nothing is ever fair, because if fairness were the basis for everything, we'd all be in deep trouble. At the same time, for reasons beyond our limited understanding, some of us face far greater hardship than others, and while that disparity is sometimes due to the choices we make, quite often choice has nothing to do with it.

So what does all of this have to do with growing up? Perhaps the best way to answer that question is to ask you what you've been feeling viscerally as you've been reading about all of these issues of fairness. When fairness is at stake, most of us are thrown back to our earliest understanding of right and wrong. But the veneration of fairness as the pinnacle of human behavior can undermine the possibility of real relationship.

Part of the reason we lust for fairness is that it seems so tidy and complete. And that's the problem. Fairness can fool us into thinking a problem is solved, but that's because ironically, when we're consumed by the Fairness Doctrine, we're usually looking at a situation from only one point of view. I have to defend my turf, because I assume you're going to defend yours. As we try to resolve our conflict, I may give some thought to what motivates your position, but if fairness is my main concern, what I'm eager to ensure, most of all, is that I get what's coming to me, and perhaps—but only perhaps—that means you'll get what's coming to you. True fairness would obviously require that, but people obsessed by fairness rarely think much about the other person.

Of course, sometimes people in conflict really are able to reach a balanced conclusion. They may resolve their differences by agreeing to meet halfway. Fairness alone will enable them to *meet*, but the only way they can truly *engage* is if each is willing to go at least a little beyond halfway—i.e., to risk going beyond what is fair. Josh and Melanie would likely have ended up going their separate ways had they resolved their differences by meeting halfway—"I'll wash the dishes if you'll be more reasonable about the alarm"—rather than each taking the risk of letting go of the petty issues in order to deal together with the more existential issues of life and death.

One of the critical distinctions between a child and an adult is the capacity for empathy. Children view the world as though they were at its center—and that's appropriate for beings entirely dependent on others. From their point of view, everything revolves around their needs and desires. Our socialization into adults, however, requires not only our willingness to acknowledge the needs and desires of others but actually to experience them as our own. That capacity, possibly unique to humans and surely the jewel in the crown of our nature, is the essence of relationship.

Nothing impedes empathy more effectively than the Fairness Doctrine. When we are consumed by the need for fairness, we give no more than we know we can get. To be sure, the introduction to children of the idea of fairness can initiate some sense of empathy. "If you take two pieces of pie, and your sister gets none, how do you think she'll feel?" But leaving it at that results in a feeble form of empathy with no appreciation of issues beyond the pie itself. Perhaps, for example, realizing she's had a rough day, you might be moved to give her the larger piece, just to help her feel better. Fairness makes no allowance for that.

Empathy is the vicarious experience of the feelings, thoughts, or attitudes of another. Without it, we fail to grow beyond ourselves; we fail to realize that the world doesn't actually revolve around us; we remain self-centered and isolated. Empathy is what makes effective human interaction possible.

Unfortunately, empathy isn't a quality that, once gained, automatically becomes a permanent habit. The truth of that statement will be clear to you if over the last few minutes you've found yourself sliding back into the Fairness Doctrine. While what we learn as small children never quite leaves us, our evolving moral consciousness enables us to overcome our childish responses. To do so, however, often requires an act of the will. Many of us have to think consciously about being empathetic in order not to revert to a more primitive response. I'm not proud of the customer service people over the years who have been the recipients of my wrath as I've attempted from time to time to get satisfaction for an incorrect charge or inadequate service or some other injustice on the part of their companies, letting my demand for fairness completely obliterate my sensitivity to the human being at the other end of the phone line.

In her deeply insightful and entertaining book, *Being Wrong: Adventures in the Margins of Error*, Kathryn Schulz notes that our attraction to certainty often makes empathy difficult if not impossible. She invites her reader to "listen to yourself the next time you argue with a family member. Leaving behind our more thoughtful and generous selves, we become smug, or patronizing, or scornful, or downright bellicose. And that's when we are fighting with people we love." [22] Righteous in our cause, we bulldoze our way over any idea, opinion, or person in our path. What empathy requires at the outset is our admission not only that we aren't certain about anything but also that we're in fact actively wrong about some things. Understanding and even confessing that flaw in ourselves is what enables us not just to tolerate but even to identify with it in others—and that's the beginning of empathy.

What empathy demands of us that a child cannot give is willing vulnerability. Children, of course, are vulnerable without willing it. You can't be *willingly* vulnerable unless you have the wherewithal *not* to be vulnerable. As we come to recognize our vulnerability, we learn strategies for defending ourselves against it. But surely one reasonable indicator of adulthood is the discerning courage, having built those defenses, to know when to let them down in order to engage fully with another human being. The Fairness Doctrine is a defensive posture. Empathy is an open stance that takes us a step beyond welcoming others into our sphere by enabling us to participate vicariously in theirs.

Not only is empathy what makes real friendship possible, it is also what makes it possible for us to resolve conflicts without resorting either to primitive violence or to mere co-existence. "You never really understand a person," says Atticus Finch to his daughter Jem in *To Kill a Mockingbird*, "until you consider things from his point of view…until you climb into his skin and walk around in it." [23] Once you've done that, it's hard to treat the other person as an irreconcilable enemy. You may not like that person any better, and you may continue to disagree with her opinions or choices. But imagining how the other person sees the world and trying to figure out why makes it difficult to remain inflexible; you learn too many complexities about the other person to persist in easy answers or rigid prejudices.

Emerson wrote in his famous essay, *Self Reliance*, "The test of a first rate intelligence is the ability to hold two opposed ideas in the mind at the same time, and still retain the ability to function." The highly mobile and information-rich lives we lead today demand not just of first-rate minds but of all of us the capacity to see gray; to understand others not as right or wrong, as good or bad, as just or unjust, but as ambiguous; to realize that the problems we face in life rarely submit to categorical solutions but are nuanced; to live, in short, with loose ends.

To become an adult is to leave behind any pretense that the world is black and white, though goodness knows, plenty of so-called adults persist in seeing the world that way. They do it by selective reasoning, choosing to believe only what supports their current positions, regardless of the level of irrationality that may require.

"Barack Obama isn't American-born." "But of course he is. He was born in Hawaii." "Well that doesn't make him American-born. Hawaii is an island." "But it's a state." "Well, he wasn't born there anyway. He was born in Indonesia." "No, he was born in Hawaii." "Prove it." "I'm sure he has a birth certificate." "Why hasn't he shown it to anyone?" "Have you seen George Bush's birth certificate?" "George Bush wouldn't have any problem showing anybody his birth certificate. He's proud to be an American. But who's ever seen Obama's birth certificate?"

That absurd dialogue is, nearly word-for-word, a conversation I had recently with a high school senior. Last summer, standing in line at a rural New Hampshire convenience store to pay for gas, I spotted a sweatshirt that said, "Don't blame me. I voted for the American." Seeing my look of dismay, the cashier exclaimed gleefully, "Fastest-selling sweatshirt in the store. Can't keep 'em in stock." My young friend is clearly not alone, and though I could argue with him for the rest of the year, I'd get nowhere. Like most of the market for that sweatshirt, he's dug into beliefs that logic won't budge. Why? President Obama represents something altogether alien to him, something to which he cannot relate, and to which he has no desire to relate. What is lacking in this young man is empathy—not just with a single human being named Barack Obama but with others with whom this young man identifies the President: Blacks, immigrants, aliens—the list is endless. They are all *others* who have no legitimate place in his universe.

My young friend's political judgments aside, I can't help worrying about how his intellectual and emotional rigidity will affect his personal future, his vocational and social choices. Right now, instead of absorbing new information and making appropriate course corrections, his mind is already closed. He's not growing. What he knows ten years from now may be little different from what he knows now; his intellectual and, to some extent, his emotional development are arrested by an atrophy of vision, so that the decisions he makes in his work and family life are likely to be, in essence, the decisions of an early adolescent.

Virtually all of us suffer from some degree of myopia—unquestioned prejudices that become a warped lens through which we view the world. Even as our bodies mature, unexamined biases stunt our minds. If our minds are to grow in sync with our bodies, we must be willing continuously to challenge what we believe to make sure we still believe it and aren't simply defending it because we don't know what else to believe.

To be an adult requires an open mind. Nothing opens our minds more effectively than deep and lasting engagement with other human beings—and, conversely, nothing closes them more effectively than isolation. Empathy is the key.

CHAPTER 6

Passion

Thirty-five years ago, I worked at a highly selective secondary school as admissions director, a position that required me to evaluate 13-year-old boys and predict what they'd be like by the time they were 18. The school was after young men who would not only excel academically but also contribute to its athletic, artistic, and social life. How do you look at a 13-year-old and figure out what he's going to turn into? In particular, how do you determine who will mature in time both to take maximum advantage of a first-rate secondary school and to become a valuable member of the community?

While standardized testing was required, it was not terribly helpful. We knew people who scored well were bright—but being bright doesn't alone guarantee maturity, motivation, dedication, leadership, and collaborative spirit—the qualities of a successful student. Teacher recommendations certainly helped, but even the teachers who knew their students well as 8th-graders were rolling the dice a bit in predicting their futures. We interviewed them all, but I was insistent as director that no one would ever be turned down solely on the basis of an interview. These kids were 13, after all; I can't remember exactly what I was like at 13, but I doubt that I would have wowed an admissions interviewer in 20 minutes.

By far the most informative part of the application was the student's personal essay. There were three things I looked for: first, the quality of the writing; second, anything distinctive about the applicant; and, third and most important, any hint of passion.

While the writing itself obviously told me about the student's linguistic ability, the nature and style of a student's written expression often gave me clues about his maturity. Facility with language has a lot to do with one's relational sensitivity. Language, after all, is one of the principal vehicles by which we relate to one another, and sophisticated writing skills often indicate someone highly attuned to other people. (Yes, parents did often edit their sons' essays, but with experience, you really can tell the difference between 8th-grade writing and parental editing.)

Distinctiveness is something of a paradox for adolescents. Most of them do all they can to be exactly like everyone else. So when we urge them to reveal what distinguishes them from everyone else, some are at a loss. The willingness to be different marks every outstanding adolescent, and it's what every secondary school and college admissions officer looks for. Difference alone, obviously, isn't enough; but it is difficult to demonstrate distinction without a willingness to be different. Best-selling author Tim Ferriss was asked recently in an interview at the Commonwealth Club of California how, with relatively poor SAT scores, he managed to get into Princeton. He responded, "In my application, I didn't try to tell them I was *better* than everyone else; I let them know I was *different* from everyone else."[24] Princeton admissions officers read more than 27,000 applications[25] for the Class of 2015 to arrive at a class of just over 1300 students.[26] Clearly, it helps one's chances to write a memorable essay. Moreover, the distinctions among applicants are what enable an admissions staff to put together an interesting and diverse class. Above all, though, admissions officers know that the willingness to distinguish oneself from the herd is a mark of the kind of maturity they seek in their applicants.

For me, though, the single most valuable quality in an applicant is passion. What I always looked for was something—almost anything—the applicant really cared about, something to which he was willing to dedicate himself. At that age, the usual passion was athletic, though certainly not always. The point wasn't to figure out who was going to be the next Bobby Orr. While athletic prowess and dedication might give me an idea of who might help our teams, I tried to focus as well on the more indirect influence such qualities might have on an applicant's long-term success. In my experience, if you find young people willing to dedicate themselves to something larger than themselves, then you are likely to see that passion blossom in other ways, as well.

Of course, people can be passionate in ways that don't advance the common good. One could be a passionate thief or passionately destructive; serial murderers are often passionate about killing. Such people's passions are directed, above all, toward themselves. What I looked for were people whose passion fueled the dreams of others, whose passions committed them to something beyond themselves, young people who despite their youth were at least subtly if not overtly inspirational. Those are the people I'd bet on every time—and while many had a stumble here or there, few of them disappointed my expectations in the long run.

You may be thinking, "Where do you find an 8th-grader like that?" But the kind of inspiration I'm talking about is something of which virtually any 8th-grader is capable. It's not a matter of extraordinary intelligence or prodigious talent; it's motivation, focus, and other-directedness. Among our applicants were star athletes, musical prodigies, science fair medalists, and essay contest winners—but these were 8th graders. Not a single star football player went on to the NFL, and the science fair medalists were as likely to become novelists as the essayists were to end up at NASA. The point of the admissions exercise was not to funnel these kids in any particular direction or to predict exactly where they'd end up but to identify who would be driven to extend his reach and who would likely work to improve the world around him.

Of all the admissions essays I've read in nearly 40 years of interviewing for colleges and secondary schools, the one that stands out was by an eighth-grader who wrote about teaching a bird to fly. The fledgling had fallen out of the nest and broken a wing. After mending the injured wing and nursing the chick for a few weeks, patiently feeding it with an eyedropper, this young man was forced, in the absence of the mother, to try to figure out how mother birds teach baby birds to fly. With the help of whatever bird books he could lay his hands on (there are no "how-to" books that teach humans to be avian mothers) and a healthy dose of intuition, he managed to pull off this little miracle. What impressed me about that essay wasn't just the qualities of imagination, determination, and care it revealed in its writer but the fact that, of all the things he could have told us about himself, that's what he chose. 35 years later, that young man is a beloved teacher of kindergarteners and first-graders, still teaching little birds how to fly, in love with his work, in love with his kids, and every bit as successful as I believed he would be. It was all in that essay.

Passion isn't easy for parents and teachers to manage. It often shows in small children as raw energy; passionate kids are the ones who wear us out. Actually, nearly all kids are passionate. You don't see many if any lazy toddlers. But as parents and teachers concentrate on helping small children develop cognitive control to balance their emotional impulsivity, sometimes passion gets smothered. It's easy to confuse impulsivity with passion and therefore to associate passion with childishness. Impulsiveness is indeed childish. But passion is child*like*—while it has its roots in our primitive nature, it is also the essence of our most mature vision.

The secret is to expose children thoughtfully to stimuli, observe carefully what attracts them, and then encourage their pursuit of passion in ways that engage their cognition, as well. For example, many children gravitate naturally to athletics as a way simply to expend energy, but some exhibit early on both natural skill and an attraction to one sport or another. Taking advantage of those physical attributes to help them think about and understand what's going on in the game is a way to merge passion and cognition, helping their natural abilities mature into something more. The advantage of merging passion and intellect is obvious in the arts, where understanding of theory, process, and nuance are essential to the refinement of raw talent.

It is certainly reasonable to encourage children to order their passions in order to prevent impulse from getting the better of them. But how do you order passion without killing it? Passion is by nature a bit chaotic, and certainly passionate people can get carried away, failing to notice the ways in which their enthusiasm can overwhelm or otherwise intrude on others and even be unintentionally destructive. The secret is not only to bring cognitive function to bear, helping children approach their passions with some analysis, but also to help them recognize the ways in which their lives and actions impact others and to learn to bring their passions to bear on behalf of others.

I tutor writing at an alternative high school program in my hometown. All of the seniors must write a 10-page research paper on topics of their choice. I'm regularly chagrinned to see how many of them initially choose topics in which they haven't the slightest interest. They assume at the outset that this exercise is going to be drudgery and seem to do everything they can to make sure it will be. When I sit down with them to talk about topics, I remind them they can write about *anything* and that there's no excuse for them to choose something in which they're not interested. They always look a bit mystified, and so I generally have to lead the way. "What do you really care about?" I recently asked Zak, who had reached a dead-end on an earlier topic. "Sports," he replied. I was a bit surprised, as I knew he didn't play on any teams. I then discovered he had sustained a head injury in an automobile accident several years earlier, and the monetary settlement in his favor carried with it the proviso that he not play varsity football or hockey, a prohibition that had been a real hardship for him, although he did tell me he intends to go into coaching and already works with younger boys as an assistant coach.

Zak's enthusiasm about sports is obvious, but when he starts talking about the kids he coaches, he becomes positively electric. He'd just never imagined he could bring that energy to bear on a school research assignment. I suggested that he might want to explore the trends of head injuries in football or hockey and the extent to which training and equipment had or had not reduced such injuries in recent years, a topic both personally relevant and useful for his future coaching plans. Zak's eyes lit up, and in no time, he was deep into the new topic.

When Josh Cooper was stuck in the printing business, he would likely have responded to the question, "What do you care about?" with a blank stare. But the secretary's mention of the suicide hotline pressed a button—here was something he had forgotten he cared about but which immediately elicited his passion—and off he went. Very shortly into his tenure in that program, Josh would have had no difficulty telling you what he cared about.

While it may be difficult for people in their late 20's casting about for what to do with their lives to recall the last time they were passionate about anything, going back may be the best way to break through their indifference and rediscover what turns them on. At every step of the way, we should be helping young people to discover what they care about, to learn to articulate it, to act in accordance with it, and continuously to rethink it.

When I was working at Princeton, the Office of the Dean of the Chapel sponsored a series of occasional talks by well-known individuals—frequently, members of the faculty, though not always—cleverly entitled, "What Matters to Me and Why." The idea was to get brilliant people like quantum physicist Freeman Dyson or psychologist and Nobel laureate Daniel Kahneman to step briefly off of their professional pedestals and share with their young audiences the motivating forces of their lives. Though the speakers were often household names or, at the least, leaders in their fields, the assignment they accepted in this talk invariably humanized them for their listeners as they publicly explored personal territory that is, or at least ought to be, the province of every human being.

What was cleverest about the title, though, lay in the subtly subversive motive of then-Dean of the Chapel Frederick Borsch, who created the series. We often identify the goals of a college education in purely intellectual terms— the development of cultural literacy, critical thinking, clear and effective writing, and proficiency in a particular area of study. But a student might gain all of that and yet miss what may be the most important aspect of development from pre- to post-adolescence: the gradual absorption, rejection, and sorting of beliefs and values that ultimately determine who we are and what we stand for. By inviting the speakers to talk about "What Matters to Me and Why," the Dean was effectively exercising his duty as pastor to the University community by encouraging the student audience to reflect on the same question.

Recently, I was involved in a group exercise in which each of us was asked to respond to a distinct, randomly selected question. One member of the group, a 25-year-old named Will, whose question was, "What makes you most anxious?" answered, "I'm most anxious right now about what I'm going to do with my life." Will is considering a variety of careers and has been thinking for some time about medicine. In the abstract, medicine seems to fit his interests. But as he looks forward to at least seven more years of training along with the unpredictable hours of a demanding medical practice, he wonders whether that profession would allow him to be the kind of husband and father he hopes to be. Listening to Will, I wondered whether he was approaching the problem backwards. He's imagining careers and trying to determine whether he fits. I suggested to him that, instead, he might focus on what he really cares about and then imagine how to build a life and career around that. The real question is, though, does he know what he cares about?

The common challenge of mid- to late-twenty-year-olds who find themselves stalled is either their inability to answer that question or their failure to focus on it in a systematic way. Hence, if we are eager to enable young people to get through their twenties without stalling, then we should establish as a goal that they be able by post-adolescence to articulate what matters to them and why. That begs the question, of course, of whether people in their early twenties have enough life experience to know. Clearly, we may not be ready at any time in our lives to say what matters to us for all time. The answer to "What Matters to Me and Why" need not be immutable in order to be both genuine and meaningful. Indeed, considering that question with an open mind forces us to allow for change in the sure knowledge that no matter how firmly grounded our values are, they will have to take account of new and perhaps transformational information. All of that said, there may be no more clearly distinguishing characteristic of adulthood than the establishment of a well-integrated set of values by which to lead and measure one's life, and it is possible, reasonable, and, I would argue, highly desirable to expect post-adolescents to be able to identify issues about which they are passionate, to be able to express that passion to themselves and others, and to have considered and be able to articulate the reasons for their passion.

What often stalls young people is a sense of powerlessness. Clearly, they are inexperienced. As they head out of school into the work world, they're fish out of water. They've spent nearly two decades learning how to negotiate school, and now they find themselves on new turf with new rules, leaving even the best of them scrambling to get their bearings. The hard-won power they used to have—leadership among their peers, respect from their teachers—now seems distant in a world in which they feel like they're starting over.

So where is their power? In their passion. To be sure, not everyone in the work world will necessarily recognize or appreciate it; but that's where their chief power lies. And the most effective way to put it to use is to figure out how they can engage their passion in work that matters.

A caveat is warranted here. I recently talked with a young man who is as eager to find his passion as he is frustrated that it remains so aloof.

Only after the end of an hour-and-a-half conversation did it occur to me that he's making the task far too difficult. What he's looking for is his life's passion, and the problem he's running into is that he's placing a time limit on a process that may in fact take a lifetime. All he needs to know today is what matters to him right now and how he can extrapolate from that a way to make himself useful. That may not sound like much, but it's a beginning—and the passion of a lifetime has to start somewhere. He's worried, of course, that starting so small may lead him down the wrong path. But his fear of walking in the wrong direction is preventing him from starting at all. What, after all, is a wrong direction? For most of us, the route to our destinies is anything but direct.

The challenge is not just figuring out who you are. It is just as much determining how others can benefit from your presence. Columnist David Brooks urged that balance in an op ed piece about commencement speeches entitled "It's Not About You":[27]

> "Today's grads enter a cultural climate that preaches the self as the center of a life. But, of course, as they age, they'll discover that the tasks of a life are at the center. Fulfillment is a byproduct of how people engage their tasks, and can't be pursued directly. Most of us are egotistical and most are self-concerned most of the time, but it's nonetheless true that life comes to a point only in those moments when the self dissolves into some task. The purpose in life is not to find yourself. It's to lose yourself."

Ironically, it is in losing ourselves that we finally gain a sense of where we are. And that enigma may be a hint about the real nature of power.

CHAPTER 7

Power, Gender, and Sexuality

More than sixty years ago, on a kindergarten playground, a bunch of my friends and I were playing King of the Hill. Before long, a girl walked over and asked, "What are you doing?" "Playing King of the Hill, " I retorted, in a tone whose subtext was, "You idiot! What do you think we're doing?" It was a game only boys played—there were no queens of the hill. She stood and watched us for a few moments, and then said with as much derision as she could muster, "That's SO stupid!"

King of the Hill combines everything we associate with being male: physicality, competitiveness, and aggressiveness. There's no way to collaborate, because there's room for only one person at the top. As a result, the game has no really satisfactory ending, because whoever wins has made a pack of enemies, each of whose goal is to replace him. The only lasting solution would be for the king to invite everyone else up to join him, but not only is there no room at the top; more to the point, Lord Acton's well-known observation about power's corrupting influence nearly always prevails. Once you're king, you tend to lose whatever interest you may ever have had in sharing the power.

If this were just a childhood game, there'd be little to worry about. Most people survive King of the Hill. Unfortunately, however, we run much of society by the same rules. And while a few women now play, and a few men think the game is stupid, we still have a long way to go before King of the Hill disappears. An astonishing number of men who inhabit the halls of Congress, the palaces of developing countries, and the towers of Wall Street have never stopped playing King of the Hill. At the epicenter of virtually every sexual scandal, economic crisis, failed state, and war is a bully flexing his muscles. Nicholas Kristof and Sheryl WuDunn argue persuasively in *Half the Sky* that most of the world's problems can be laid to the oppression of women, and that if we simply attended to women's equality, even some of our most intractable issues would evaporate.[28] How better to support the equality of women than to find a way to help the boys who are running much of the world to grow up? What would the world look like if men respected women—and respected the feminine side of themselves? If they learned to share power and authority? If they truly understood that, try as they might, there's no way to get rid of that x-chromosome and that, indeed, it's worth valuing?

For at least 10,000 years across the vast majority of the world's cultures, the domination of males has determined gender roles, personality, and relationships that, until surprisingly recently, have served to preserve patriarchy. "Surprisingly," because democracy is more than 2500 years old, and yet no one thought to include women until Sweden permitted tax-paying women to vote in 1718. (Unfortunately, Swedish women lost that privilege in 1771.) [29] While women in what was then the British colony of New Zealand could vote in 1893, they couldn't run for legislative office until 1919.[30] American women didn't obtain general suffrage, of course, until the 19th Amendment passed in 1920.

Whether Jefferson really intended "All men are created equal" to be gender-exclusive, the priority of men in American society prevailed for more than two centuries after the proclamation of what most Americans now acknowledge, at least cognitively if not viscerally, to be universal equality, and perhaps most remarkable, the inherent contradiction was lost on nearly everyone. Only after the mid-twentieth century and the introduction of efficient and convenient birth control methods were women finally free to explore the possibilities of full equality. Thus was Women's Liberation born.

It's easy to forget that Women's Liberation is just four decades old and must still fight tooth and nail for all of its gains. While both houses of Congress passed the Equal Rights Amendment in 1972, it has yet to be ratified by the required two-thirds of the states, though the movement has been sufficiently effective to threaten those who have pinned their identities on male dominance—and that group is by no means just men. Phyllis

Schlafly, the most prominent female opponent of the ERA, represents a large group of women who are perfectly willing to trade equality for what they perceive to be the stability and comfort provided by a world dominated by men. At the same time, not only in the United States and other Western cultures but even more dramatically in developing countries, where patriarchy remains very much alive if not necessarily well, men in charge are often reluctant to share the power they have held alone for so long. Indeed, sharing power seems antithetical to the highly aggressive and competitive male personality that patriarchy has encouraged. It doesn't take a Ph.D. in anthropology, sociology, or psychology to recognize the social and psychic dysfunction bred by the substantial imbalance of power between men and women for the last ten millennia.

If there is such a thing as historical destiny, however, history's moral arc, to paraphrase Dr. King, is bent toward equality. And yet we should not underestimate the social and psychological turmoil wrought by the dramatic transformation of society through which we are now living. Everyone's role is changing. No longer do men go to work while women stay home. Everyone is expected to work; everyone is expected to raise a family and do housework. Women run companies; men are stay-at-home dads. As the balance of power shifts, we are discovering that traits we had always associated with men or women turn out not to be gender-related but determined instead by who has the power. Women are just as capable as men at leading, and men really can clean a bathroom. No doubt there are traits that are truly gender-linked, but the power imbalance has misled us about what they are. And what many people, both men and women, are discovering in this new world we are in the midst of creating is a kind of wholeness of which the former division of labor deprived us. Men are coming to acknowledge and value within themselves what they formerly rejected and feared as feminine, and women are similarly willing to claim authority in ways that, just a few years ago, they would have been afraid would make them terminally unattractive to men.

Some things haven't changed, of course, and don't seem likely to. As men still can't give birth or nurse babies, equality of opportunity continues to be complicated by practical issues of biology like ticking biological clocks. On the other hand, since the work week was initially organized for men's convenience, women are learning to demand and men, to provide, creative work options like flex time, parental leave, and electronic communities that still allow for full collaboration and don't deprive women of "tenure-track" positions.

The blurring of difference between men and women, refreshing in a great many ways though it may be, is bound to leave us all at least a bit mystified. And compounding the problem is that, as clarity of gender identity disappears, so does clarity of sexual identity. As both the Women's Movement and the AIDS epidemic began to give gays the courage to be open about their sexuality, stereotypes began to fall away, and gradually, new definitions of sexuality have taken hold. As with gender, sexuality is coming to be defined individually, with all of us falling somewhere on a continuum between hetero- and homosexuality. People have begun to lose their fear of honest exploration and to be willing to confess feelings that heretofore have been taboo.

Thus do today's college students find themselves in a world their parents would barely recognize, invited to identify themselves as or at least provide moral support for lesbians, gays, transsexuals, bisexuals, asexuals, the transgendered, and everything in between. If there is no requirement to "declare," as with an academic major, the process of negotiating psychological and social life as an adolescent does nevertheless require at the least some self-understanding about where one is on the gender and sexuality spectra, and the possibilities are infinite. Moreover, while today's enlightenment is light years from where we were just a generation ago, the fact that we're still arguing publicly about the rights of the 12% or more of our society who are not heterosexual bears sad witness to the pain we continue to inflict on those outside the mainstream—even a broadening mainstream—as they attempt to grow into their sexuality.

Revolutions don't happen overnight, and what makes them so painful and destructive is that those who stand to benefit from the status quo are often prepared to fight to the death—especially if it's someone else's death. We are witnessing around the globe what history will surely record as the last gasp of the Old Order—the system of male dominance that has prevailed for so long. While we have just finished the bloodiest century in history, the current one may well eclipse it unless we figure out how to stop playing the increasingly lethal game of King of the Hill.

Not many young men imagine themselves leading countries, although some will lead companies, and a few will run for office. But every relationship is marked by its particular balance of power, and those young men whose identities continue to depend on holding the hill are likely to have difficulty recognizing the equality of those they think may threaten that position. It is surely no accident that, as women achieve increasing numbers and authority on college campuses, some men have simply hardened in their defense of male dominance. According to the Centers for Disease Control, 20-25% of US college women are the victims of rape or attempted rape during college[31]—and given the generally accepted assumption that sexual assaults are substantially underreported, the actual percentage of victims is likely much higher. Sexual assault is far more about power than about sex. The rapist is saying to his victim, in essence, "You may think what's yours is yours, but I want it, and I'm going to take it. I'm King of the Hill." That 90% of the rapists of college women are acquaintances of their victims[32] suggests that many of the perpetrators don't even know what they are doing is criminally wrong—or at least manage to convince themselves that it isn't. Especially frightening is the magnification of male power in cases of gang rape, when mob rule takes over and any semblance of adult behavior completely disappears.

Clearly, not every male college student turns into a rapist, but given the rampant statistics, chances are, he will know someone who is, though he may well not be aware of it. That fact alone places nearly every college male—even the most caring and sensitive of them—in a culture that both endangers and humiliates women. Of course, all of these observations are equally true of the victimization of those whose sexual orientation continues to place them at risk. Such an environment is mutually destructive of perpetrator and victim, and of the bystanders, as well. Everyone's humanity is undermined.

So what do we do about this seemingly endless game that no one can possibly win? Perhaps we should discourage people from playing it in the first place. But that will require a radical transformation of our society, which author Christopher Lasch aptly named in his memorable 1979 book title, *A Culture of Narcissism*.[33] In our eagerness for our children to succeed, we often make the mistake of feeding their egos instead of their spirits. We define their success as a zero-sum game, a competition rather than a collaboration. We urge them toward positions of power over others; far more rarely do we teach them the value—to themselves and those around them—of empowering others. Pushing our children to be King of the Hill may not turn them all into monsters, but it will likely undermine their sensitivity and compassion, their capacity for constructive relationships, their realistic assessment of themselves, their sense of boundaries, and the likelihood of their achieving even a modicum of humility.

We may seem to have left the realm of gender and sexuality, but it is our society's constricted understanding of those categories that has gotten us into this trouble in the first place. And while the ambiguity of gender and sexual identity may complicate our lives, it holds the promise of enriching our identities as well as our relationships.

There is considerable focus these days on encouraging women and girls to claim their authority, know their value, assert their rights. But we need to focus on men and boys, as well. As they're the ones who still have the bulk of the power, they are in the best position to alter the equation. The Million Man March in 1995, whose purpose was to encourage men to take responsibility for their families and be better husbands and fathers, was directed primarily at the African American community. What we need is a movement equivalent to Women's Liberation to liberate men and boys from their limited sense of themselves so that both men and women may take their rightful places in society and become fully realized as human beings.

By their very disjunction from the age in which we live, outmoded stereotypes can provide the impetus for both females and males to explore more broadly and deeply the nuances of gender and sexuality. As in virtually every other aspect of who we are, we are beginning to discover that, even with respect to gender and sexuality, each of us is unique. Even as that uniqueness beckons each of us to self-discovery, however, it also reminds us that none of us fits very well into any category. Our tendency to identify people as insiders or outsiders, either relieved to be included among the former or afraid of being relegated to the latter, really doesn't make much sense if everyone is truly unique. Of course, preoccupation with our own singularity can become an exercise in navel-gazing. But the corollary recognition that everyone else is just as exceptional is the requisite step toward honoring one another's equality. And honoring one another's equality becomes the basis for our understanding that our identities as human beings aren't discrete, one from another, but inextricably bound.

There's a Bantu word for it, *ubuntu*, which expresses people's interconnectedness—the way in which our lives, our personalities, and, indeed, our very being flows into and out of those around us. That each of us is unique and yet indefinable without the rest of us is the human paradox that makes the quest for identity both fascinating and elusive. It also completely redefines power. What's the point of being King of the Hill if all of those people you're dominating from your perch are, in fact, part of who you are? You've won the game not just at their expense but at your own, as well. Becoming King of the Hill is always a pyrrhic victory, because the winners lose at least as much as they win. And perhaps their greatest loss is that most of them remain unaware that they've lost anything at all.

What, then, is success? In a world that recognizes true equality, that promotes collaboration and the sharing of power and authority, what gives people a legitimate sense of achievement? What, in such a world, does it mean to lead?

What it doesn't mean, certainly, is to dominate. No, to lead in a world that honors the equality of all is to *empower* others.

Such a definition of success makes it equally accessible to all—male or female, gay or straight, poor or rich. We all have the capacity to empower, sometimes in small ways, sometimes in large. The will to empower others is an antidote to our culture of narcissism and the engine of effective community. And yet even as the vector of power points away from us, nothing makes us feel more powerful than effectively empowering someone else. Power used that way turns out to be a renewable resource. Unlike power we reserve to ourselves, it is not subject to the "zero-sum" principle. The more we use power in the service of others, the more we have. Unlike King of the Hill, everybody wins.

Growing up isn't a matter of gaining power. It's figuring out how to harness and use the power we've always had. The power to create, to encourage, to build, to bind, to care, and to love—that power is infinite, and yet it is within everyone's province. Growing up is recognizing that the only power that matters is the power we can give away, and then committing ourselves to do just that.

CHAPTER 8

Finding a Sense of Direction

Socrates says in *The Apology*, "The unexamined life is not worth living." Because we are responsible for making decisions, it isn't enough simply to *live* life; we need to consider it, stand back from it, analyze and interpret it. If passion is the driver of our lives, what we believe is what governs our passion and gives it structure and balance. Passion without belief is raw, undisciplined, and unconsidered emotion and, as such, can be unruly and dangerous. When we reflect upon it, question it, and subject it to moral scrutiny, however, passion can become the engine of our creative being. Passion is to a large extent involuntary—a compelling, driving force— whereas belief is intentional, the system of ethical judgment that governs our passion. If passion without belief lacks a rational center, though, belief without passion is lifeless. The depressed young man casting about for a purpose in life needs most of all to get in touch with his passion. That's what the suicide hotline did for Josh Cooper. It awakened in him a drive that until then had lain largely dormant. As he completes his degree in crisis counseling, his passion has been tempered by reflection. It is still at least as strong, but it is now more focused and articulated. That's the kind of balance of which I think Socrates would have approved.

While a long tradition in religion associates belief with creedal state- ments, I am generally suspicious of what people *say* they believe. I'm even suspicious of what *I* say I believe. Some of what I say I believe is what I'd like to believe, what I attain to, but what I rarely achieve. Worse than simply falling short, people sometimes espouse beliefs that have little to do with who they really are. I think of fundamentalist clergy who rail against homosexuality and then get caught in compromising relationships that belie their preaching. What we actually believe often doesn't line up with what we say we believe; real belief is less about what we say than about how we truly feel, what we do, where we stand.

Belief and *faith* are words most people identify with religion, but all of us act out of faith, whether religious or not. Faith is simply belief in a proposition that can't be proven. That none of us can know everything forces us all to depend quite a lot on faith. Some of our faith has become unconscious—e.g., that the sun will continue to rise and set. (Well, that's not what's really happening, is it? That just shows you how wayward our faith can be!) But I am eager here to focus on conscious faith—the accumulation of identified principles that serve as the backdrop for all of our decisions.

Many people envy those who are deeply religious, assuming they have somehow cornered the market on the truth. It may be a surprising thing for a priest to confess, but what religious people gain from faith is not necessarily the truth—some may, some may not, and it's impossible to prove who is who; no, what both religious and non-religious people gain from whatever it is they believe in is a compass, a sense of direction provided by principles that, together, give them a kind of logic about their lives—a quality otherwise known as *integrity*, i.e., the essence of a well-*integrated* personality. Having thought through some of life's thorny issues and arrived, even tentatively, at some conclusions about them, they are able to use their faith as a map to help them make decisions when they find themselves at a fork in the road.

My son Justin recently made such a decision—not earthshaking, but still the kind of decision people his age regularly face, some more successfully than others. The organization for which Justin works had just chosen him to run one of its satellite programs. As an avocation, he had participated with a group of college friends in the start-up of a small craft brewery, and simultaneously with his promotion, the brewery seemed poised to take off, requiring more of his time and commitment. In addition, he was about to get married. Some people wouldn't even recognize that this situation called for a choice; they'd just let it all happen and then wonder why they soon became overwhelmed. Recognizing before anyone else that trying to do all three might result in a train wreck, Justin spent time thinking about what he considers most important. He loves his job, does it well, and cares deeply about the people he serves—he certainly wasn't going to let the brewing business eat into any of that. Where he might have fudged was his marriage, because most of us figure we can get away with taking for granted the people we love most. It would have been easy to say to his future wife, "This is temporary; we can manage it for a while, right?" But as the preciousness of his marriage is at the very top of Justin's list of guiding principles, and right behind that is the principle that says, "If you're going to do it, you need to be committed," his "faith" led him to withdraw from the brewery.

We often make the assumption that knowing the difference between right and wrong is somehow instinctive. Even the law assumes adults know right from wrong, using that standard to determine the basis for an insanity plea or whether to try people as juveniles. But the concrete choices with which we are faced are rarely so obvious. None of us has the luxury of being able to float through life thoughtlessly, letting decisions essentially make themselves. Those who do generally pay a high price, at least in the long run, as their unconsidered choices turn out to have consequences for which they are altogether unprepared.

Thus do we return to the encouragement by Socrates that we examine our lives. Many people go blissfully along with an altogether unconscious faith, but the price they pay for that is that their decisions are controlled largely by unconscious beliefs or even unrestrained passions; as conscious beings, they are barely making decisions at all. If they tried to drive across the country the way they drive through their lives, they'd soon be hopelessly lost—which, in fact, is pretty much where they are.

Now even I, a priest, recognize that faith can lead people astray and often has. Paradoxically, faith serves us best when we remain sufficiently open-minded to question what we believe in. The give and take of interior debate about faith is what keeps it vital. Our lives, after all, are constantly changing, and we are bombarded with new information continuously. What we believe in needs to take account of that new information. When faith becomes rigid, new information tends to bounce off, and though it may render our faith obsolete and irrelevant, we'll have no way of knowing it. The choice, though, isn't between rigid faith and nothing at all. Mature reflection can help us arrive at principles that make room for information that, at least for now, doesn't quite fit into our world view—i.e., facts we can neither make complete sense of nor ignore. Whether our faith or guiding principles are religious or not, they must be the product of serious reflection if we are to be in any meaningful way the drivers of our destiny.

But let's face it: reflection is simply not an American habit. Writing in 1840, Alexis De Toqueville, the quintessential Ameriphile, wrote, "I think that in no country in the civilized world is less attention paid to philosophy than in the United States."[34] True, life here is fast-paced and prone to sensory overload, conditions that might well discourage reflection. But more to the point is that Americans by our very nature are *doers*.

What's the first thing we Americans ask each other after being introduced? "What do you do?" That's how most of us define ourselves—by what we do. Now, Americans aren't alone in that, nor is this a new custom. The very fact that many of our names are derived from the vocations of our ancestors suggests that *doing* has long been closely associated with identity. Of course, the question, "What do you do?" can be an unfortunate way to try to begin a friendship in the kind of economy in which we currently find ourselves, when so many are out of work. How do you respond confidently to "What do you do?" if you've just lost your job?

It strikes me that a more appropriate question—though one that is hard to imagine at the average cocktail party—would be, "Who are you?" Then the respondent can reply as she wishes: I am Melanie Cooper; I am a mother; I am a wife; I am a teacher; I am a violinist; I am a birdwatcher; I am a sometime skier; I am a cancer survivor; I'm concerned about global warming; I am a domestic violence responder; I am excited about my son's upcoming hockey game; I am sad that my father died recently. The possibilities are endless. One could reasonably ask whether we really want to know so much about each other on first introduction, but given the worth our culture places on extroversion, I don't believe standoffishness is what keeps us from sharing at a deeper level. The more likely cause is the priority we place on action over thought, an inclination of national temperament that has earned us the sobriquet "can-do Americans." But being "can-do" doesn't mean we can't think.

I have no wish to suggest that institutional religion is the only or in all cases the best venue for determining what is true and what matters. But the quest for meaning is, for everyone, a spiritual matter, regardless of how they choose to define it or pursue it. And while it may be true that Americans as a group are not prone to reflection, many young people are hungry to know who they are and how they fit into the universe.

One of the very satisfying aspects of my work as a college chaplain was that, though I lacked faculty credentials, I was always made to feel, by faculty and students alike, that what I did was important. That wasn't so much a comment on me as on the value many in the community placed on the spiritual needs of students. It never ceased to amaze me that, at the unlikely hour of 10 o'clock on a Sunday night, 60-80 students regularly showed up for Episcopal services, rather than study, have a beer with friends, or go to bed. Why? For some, it was just a matter of habit—they'd always done it. But most were simply searching and found in that quiet hour a fellowship that welcomed searchers. I'd love to be able to tell you it was my preaching, and I do from time to time get letters or emails from former students reminding me of a sermon that meant a lot to them. Most of the time, however, I can't remember having said what they attribute to me and assume the words are theirs, not mine, nonetheless grateful that their faulty memories now give me credit for the inspiration. I think it is frequently true, in any case, that when people come to a service with issues on their minds, they hear more in the sermon than the preacher may ever have intended, and there's nothing wrong with that. The point isn't for the listener to be able to pass an exam on the sermon; the point is that the spirit of the listener be enriched, however that happens, and frequently, listeners are more active participants in the sermon than they realize. That's how the reflective process works.

The chaplaincy met, as well, on Wednesday evenings at Procter House, our home and the chaplaincy headquarters, for communion, dinner, and discussion, often with a guest speaker, but always on a topic that sought to help the students make sense of the world through a spiritual lens. For many, those were the sessions in which they wrestled the issues to the ground. But beyond the substance of those evenings was the fact that they happened—that once a week, students crossed the street, leaving behind the campus world, and entered a home with kids and dogs, a place where many of them felt grounded. It was a sufficient counterpoint to their lives on campus to pull them out of themselves a bit and encourage them to take on the big questions.

And given half a chance, students today will take on the big questions. Recently, an organization called the Veritas Forum held a debate at Bowdoin College. According to the event program, "The Veritas Forum was started at Harvard in 1992 by a group of students, faculty, and ministers…as a response to an emptiness on campus." The topic of the debate was, "What does it mean to be good? Two scholarly perspectives, Christian and secular," and the speakers were a philosophy professor from Bowdoin (the secularist) and the associate director of the Rivendell Institute, a Christian research institute at Yale. The moderator was a popular Bowdoin government professor. Now I should add that, though Bowdoin's main campus has been dominated since 1855 by a large chapel with a pair of looming towers and a bell that chimes four times an hour, all of which make its presence inescapable, Bowdoin has never had a chaplain and is one of the least overtly religious campuses I know of. So I went to the Veritas Forum expecting a handful of people, mostly other adults from town, and was astonished instead to find the auditorium so packed with students that a seat on the floor in the aisle was difficult to find. Well over 10% of the student body had come on a Thursday night—usually a party night as Friday is a light class day for many—to hear what it means to be good from a Christian and a secular point of view. (The Christian speaker appropriately broadened his approach to "theistic," rather than exclusively Christian, sensitively opening the conversation to the entire audience.) The debate was high-level, the questions pointed and thoughtful, and if there had been any doubt, it was more than clear that night that reflection is alive and well at Bowdoin College.

Unfortunately, there are a great many young people who don't find themselves in communities that support that kind of reflection, and at least in part because of their lack of contact with people outside their own age group, they are not impelled to think about such things. As a result, they head into their middle twenties with no sense of who or where they are. It's clearly too late for them to re-do college, but it's not too late to get them focused on the questions they need to be asking themselves.

The compass is the place to begin with a young person who is at odds about the next step to take. "What do you value? What do you believe in? And how does that inform what you care about?" If there's any daylight between what they say they care about and what they plan to do, ask them why. Because if you can get people to let go of the external demands for a moment—salary and lifestyle expectations, other people's definition of success, their anxiety about time, even what seems possible—so that they can dream a little and actually let their passion and principles take flight, they may be able to discern a vocation. Vocation isn't just a job, after all— it's literally a calling. When you help a young person ask the big questions about herself, you unmuffle her inner voice, and perhaps she'll be able to hear it.

CHAPTER 9

Vocation

Years ago, a teaching colleague of mine upbraided me for my ongoing concern about the extent to which I was fulfilling what I was called to do. "What is it about you clergy," he grumbled. "You guys are always talking about 'being called.' The rest of us just have jobs." In fact, I thought then and continue to believe my friend was dead wrong. I am convinced that everyone has a *vocation* or calling, a purpose in being here, and I believe that purpose—whom we're meant to be and what we're meant to do—is constituted in our spiritual DNA and is as unique for each of us as the rest of our personal genome.

Where my friend went astray, as most people do, is in identifying "vocation" with "job." Our jobs are what we get paid for. Vocation is far broader—it is about what we're meant to do with our whole lives, and that involves far more than our salaried employment. It really includes our every waking moment. Remember, vocation is about not just *what we do* but *who we are*. But what is the source of vocation? Whose voice is doing the calling? That's not an easy question to answer, and certainly not everyone will agree on the nature of the voice. But I think we can at least find some identifying features of true vocation that can help us determine whether the voice we are hearing is legitimate.

Earlier, I described my own journey toward teaching that began during my junior year of college. But I left out some important details, because I wanted then to focus on dealing with failure. The subject of vocation leads me to revisit that journey, because vocation is what it was all about. And my own experience of calling, as it turns out, was pretty extraordinary.

When I decided I wasn't cut out to write film scores, I had a problem. For the first time in my life, I hadn't the slightest idea what to do with my life. I had always known. In high school, I was going to be an architect. In college, I was going to be a composer. Now, I was totally at sea. Perhaps to postpone the evil day when I'd have to make a definitive decision, I made an appointment with the Dean of Admission at Princeton to ask him whether I might be able to work in the Admission Office after I graduated. As I had run the student guide service, we had gotten to know each other reasonably well, so I thought I at least had a shot. I wasn't prepared for his response: "I think there might be a possibility of that. But I should tell you I'd never hire anyone for admissions who isn't interested in secondary school teaching."

Secondary school teaching? The idea had frankly never occurred to me, and at first blush, it didn't excite me. But I did begin to wonder why someone interested in secondary school teaching would want to be an admission officer. Teachers, after all, have long-term relationships with their students and are presumably attracted to that aspect of teaching. Admission officers meet applicants for 20 minutes (if they are fortunate enough actually to interview them) and know them only on paper after that. The more I thought about it, the less sense it made. Admissions would surely be extremely frustrating for someone who wanted to be a teacher.

This conundrum continued to bother me, and gradually I realized it wasn't only teachers who might find admissions work frustrating; it began to dawn on me that such work might be deeply frustrating for me—because, like the teachers I was imagining, I have always prized my long-term relationships, especially with young people. All of this reflection finally came to a head one day when, walking across campus, I was suddenly brought involuntarily to a dead halt. To this day, I remember exactly where I was, though the path was rerouted years ago. What stopped me in my tracks was the utterly astonishing revelation that I was going to be a teacher. Not that I might be a teacher, or that I ought to think about being a teacher, or even that there was a likelihood of my becoming a teacher; no, what I suddenly *knew* beyond the shadow of a doubt was that I was *going* to be a teacher. There was no Charlton Heston voice commanding me, no writing in the sky of the sort that inspired Charlemagne, but I *knew*, nevertheless. And perhaps most amazing was that my immediate reaction was to cry, out loud, "What? I don't want to be a teacher." But even as I momentarily balked, I realized that was what I was going to be. It wasn't as though I were being forced against my will; I could still choose to ignore the voice. But it seemed silly to do so inasmuch as it was so clear that this is what I was meant to do.

"You are going to be a teacher" is the first thing in my life I ever truly *knew*. So how did I know it? As a priest, of course, I'm inclined to talk about this experience in transcendent terms, and I do continue to believe personally that this was a divine revelation. (And by the way, whether you think of the voice as coming from beyond or from within doesn't really resolve whether it's divine. It may come from what psychiatrist Carl Jung referred to as the "collective unconscious," the deepest part of our personal unconscious that connects with the unconscious of the culture and may in fact be divine.) But if that sort of talk makes you uncomfortable, let me assure you that I don't think it's necessary to see it in those terms in order to give legitimacy to the experience. What I think happened that made that moment accessible to me, whether it was divine or not, was a merging of the most important forces in my life at that moment, a synchronizing of virtually all of the significant issues I was considering. That unanticipated synthesis of sense, thought, emotion, and intuition whose interaction had up to then produced such chaos in my mind was uniquely compelling and, not surprisingly, took hold of me. Perhaps it was the sheer elegance of it all—the way everything in my life suddenly fit—that led me so willingly to submit to so unexpected a vision.

My life has taken a good many surprising turns since that spring day in 1966, but the impulse to be a teacher has been at the heart of it all. Indeed, it is even what is driving this book. But I can hear you saying, "That's fine for you. But what about those of us who have never been struck by a thunderbolt and doubt that we ever will?"

I've shared this story not because I think everyone is likely to have a similar experience but to let you know such things do happen and may in fact happen to you. That said, though, it is certainly true for me and likely true for you that revelations about whom we're meant to be are usually far more subtle. Either way, what we should all be looking for is that coalescing of forces in our lives that gives us a sense of consistency. What happened to me happened in part because I was asking lots of questions and, for the first time in my life, open to whatever answers came my way. Not that I had become totally mindless; I was simply trying to cast off old preconceptions in order to make room for things I'd never thought about before. And without being altogether conscious of it, I was on a quest for coherence, in part because my life had become somewhat incoherent—I didn't know where I was going; once again, we're back to that old-fashioned word *integrity*, i.e., the condition of being fully integrated.

When young people ask, "What should I do with my life?" they are often tempted to look at potential careers and determine whether they can shoehorn themselves in. There are two problems with that approach. First, careers are interesting, but human beings, infinitely more so. Using a potential career instead of all of the creative energy within us as the inspiration for how to shape our lives is likely to lead us to ignore important things about ourselves as we try to jam the irregular puzzle pieces we are into the pre-cut shapes future careers may offer us. Careers tend to provide generic opportunities, but none of us is generic.

Second, as we think about what we're meant to do with our lives, we need to be thinking about a lot more than our careers. We need to think about family life, parenting, our "extra-curricular" lives, our philanthropic lives, our lives as citizens, our spiritual lives—in short, we need to consider our whole selves. A helpful if somewhat sobering exercise is to write the obituary you would love to have earned by the time you die; it probably won't just talk about what a great banker or lawyer or CEO you were.

The search for what to do with our lives is far more an internal than an external quest, and necessarily so if we are to discover the callings that are distinctively our own. Just as no two people are identical, no two people have the same callings in life. Scores of books like the time-honored *What Color Is Your Parachute?*[35] provide help with the question, but only to the extent that they guide us back to ourselves as the answer. To be sure, part of the process of discerning vocation involves a sober assessment of the costs and benefits of any career one is considering. But the far more difficult judgment for most of us is the honest assessment of our own desires, demands, impulses, and goals.

That judgment is often skewed by forces to which we give more weight than we should. Some fall prey to the pressure of parents who, attempting to live out their own ambitions through their children, urge them into lives they aren't meant to live. Others focus on the apparent perks of a career. "I've always wanted to be a doctor, because for as long as I can remember, the person I've most admired was our family doctor. He led the life I'd like to lead. Respected in the community, he has a wonderful family, belongs to the country club, and lives the good life. That's what I want." Of course, none of that has anything to do with medicine. Imagine grinding out four years of pre-med, another four years of medical school, and three to six years of residency, only to discover that medicine is no longer practiced the way it used to be, and that if indeed you've managed by chance to find anything to like about the career of medicine itself, you're working so hard just to pay your malpractice insurance that there's little time for your family and less for the country club you may not be able to afford.

Still others are more realistic about the careers they're considering but gravitate to them from a misguided understanding of success. "I am going to be an investment banker because I need to make my first million by the time I'm 35." Maybe he will, and maybe he won't, but chances are, even if he does, he won't view the achievement as success once he gets there. It was John D. Rockefeller who, when asked, "How much money is enough?" reportedly replied, "Just a little bit more." Even those who look beneath the surface to confirm their success still often measure themselves against the wrong standards. "My dad was running his own company by the time he was 40. I want to beat that mark." He is not his dad. There is no timeline engraved in stone anywhere that says if he doesn't move faster through life than his father did, he will be a failure. He has imposed that judgment upon himself.

We are doomed to failure if we model our dreams on the success of others. Our only chance at success is to be ourselves. As we seek to know what to do with our lives, there is simply no alternative to listening for the voice that helps us discover the unique human beings we are and are intended to become. It's the voice that tells us what we believe in. It reminds us of what we know to be right from wrong (sometimes when we wish it wouldn't). It compels us toward our moral commitments. It pushes us beyond ourselves to care for others and the world around us. Above all, it cries out to us, "You matter. You can make a difference." But it's easy for that authentic voice to become smothered by other voices that arise from the worst rather than the best of who we are—the one that encourages us to take short cuts, the one that urges us to think first of ourselves because no one else will, the cynical voice that erodes our confidence in what is best about ourselves and others, that drives us to give up on ourselves and try to be someone else.

I've said nothing here about skills. Responding to our appropriate vocation clearly requires honesty with ourselves about what we are and are not good at. But skill level can be a trap, leading us to do what we're good at even though we're not particularly compelled by it, or leading us away from what may be challenging, though our passion for it might help us meet the challenge. I went to college planning to be an architect. I had worked for two architects during high school, was excited about the field, and seemed to have some conceptual talent. But I have had a life-long tremor in my hands that undermined my ability to draw, would have made all-night drafting sessions a nightmare and, at the least, cast doubt on my future as an architect. (CAD, of course, wasn't an option in 1963.) I finally faced facts and decided a career in architecture was simply not in the cards. But that decision my freshman year didn't prevent me as an adult from designing one house and substantially redesigning two others. Our paid jobs are not the only way of living out our dreams.

How do we hear the authentic voice? It doesn't always speak a language we instantly understand, nor does it always tell us what we want to hear. We have to be creative about interpreting messages around us that tell us who we are. How many times do friends and colleagues have to say to us things like, "You know, you're a terrific listener," or "When are you going to write a book?" (as a good friend of mine has asked insistently) before we figure out that we're meant to use that skill in a more vital way in our lives. The voice doesn't always "speak" at all. The inability to get through the day without sitting down at the piano may not be a sign that you ought to con-sider a concert career, but you'd better be sure the life you plan leaves you ample opportunity to play. If political activism has been important and satisfying for you, you may or may not want to head for a political career, but you'll certainly want to be sure to develop some means of pursuing the causes you believe in.

The challenge is to consider our whole lives in advance with the humil-ity to recognize that we're not very good at predicting the future, nor are we always very astute at hearing or understanding our inner voice. As a college chaplain aware that my young charges wanted to be able to plan out their future lives to the minute, I used to advise them to "leave room for God's surprises." That advice is born of personal experience. Very little of what has happened to me over the 45 years since I graduated from college was remotely apparent my freshman year. But the voice was always there, and the unfolding events of my life began to amplify it. Fortunately, I gradually got better at listening.

Growing up, finally, is getting into sync with ourselves, with all we are meant to be; coming to terms with our limits and possibilities, and transcending ourselves as we reach out in relationship to others. Those are the challenges to which the mature and fulfilling life calls each of us.

Chapter 10

Parenting for Adulthood

First, a disclaimer: I am not an expert parent. There are no expert parents. I've known incredible parents with screwed-up kids, and incredible kids with screwed-up parents. It's not that good parenting makes no difference; only that there's a lot of dumb luck in the outcome. The difference between a juvenile delinquent and a future Rhodes Scholar can sometimes be nothing more than who got caught. Oh yes, the odds certainly favor the child brought up in a stable, two-parent home with plenty of resources, a solid sense of values, and lots of love. But statistics are about group averages, not individuals, and fortunately for individuals, anything is possible.

What I say here is based on nothing more or less than my personal observations from nearly 40 years of ministry and 73 years of parenting of children who are now 26, 25, and 22. (Ok, some might say that's only 26 years of parenting, since, after all, the terms were concurrent—but it certainly seems like 73.) As no two parents are alike any more than any two children are alike, I'm not prepared to claim that my conclusions are applicable to everyone's experience. But because both the intense competition among many American parents and the closely guarded privacy of many modern American families sometimes make it hard for parents to talk openly about their challenges, perhaps what I share here can at least reassure other parents that what they're going through may not be unique.

I should also say that, while parents clearly are the most significant influence in most children's lives, we are not quite as important as we'd either like to think or are afraid we might be. A wise psychiatrist once said to me, "*All* parents are at least a little bit neurotic. But fortunately, most children are pretty resilient and manage to survive our mistakes." More than a few times, while confessing some misjudgment we made as parents, my wife and I have said to our children ruefully, "You know, you didn't come with directions. We're doing the best we can." Occasionally, we'd at least take credit for giving them something to tell their therapists when they're 40. But clearly, no one has a better opportunity than parents to influence our children's maturation favorably.

So if, as I suggested at the outset, the essence of adulthood is embracing the limits of one's mortality and learning one isn't the center of the universe, then what can parents do to ensure that their children gain such enlightenment? How, in other words, do we effectively encourage our kids to become adults?

The relationship between parents and their children is unique, but as obvious as that observation may seem on its face, the single biggest mistake parents can make is to forget to be parents. Their obligation not to do so is dictated by the inherent imbalance in the relationship. Parents, after all, have made a choice that resulted in the birth of their children. Even surprise pregnancies are the result of parental choice, though the parents may not have realized what they were choosing at the time. Children, on the other hand, exercise no choice in their birth, and while life may be a blessing, it is certainly not a chosen blessing. That crucial distinction places upon parents the moral responsibility to care for their children; children are under no such reciprocal obligation—at least as long as they are children.

Almost no one would argue with that observation. Yet even the unconscious unwillingness to acknowledge the special and unreciprocated responsibility of parents may be the single most damaging failure of dysfunctional parents. Love-starved teen mothers look to their babies to give the love they've been unable to find elsewhere. Dads look to their sons to be the pals their busy mobile lives prevent them from finding among peers. Unappreciated moms searching in vain for some authority in the family look to their daughters to buoy their confidence. Ambitious parents look to their children to succeed on their behalf. Parents of troubled teens, afraid their children won't like them, side with their children against authorities rather than holding them accountable. Single parents look to children as emotional substitutes for the missing partner. Children are neither pets nor surrogate adults; they lack the resources to meet their parents' needs, and, more to the point, their status as children means they have needs of their own for which they depend on their parents. People who have children to fill holes in their own lives—and more than a few do—need to rethink that plan.

Do parents and children ever "graduate" from that unbalanced relationship? Can they be friends? Of course. Nothing pleases me more than that our three kids have become our best friends—but not because we tried to make that happen, and not because we needed it to happen. We have friends. They have friends. We don't *need* one another for friendship. Our friendship grew naturally as we began to relate as adults, and we have been able to relate as adults because, when they needed us to be parents, we were parents. And much as we enjoy our adult relationships with our kids, they still need us to be parents from time to time.

The single most important requirement of parents, and the one that by its very nature cannot expect reciprocity, is that they love their children unconditionally. That means loving them when they are unable or unwilling to love us back; it means loving them when they seem most unlovable. That may sound like a tall order. Parents will not always like their children, after all, but whether or not we like them in a given moment is beyond our control. All of them, at one time or another, will do things that make us angry, disappoint us, even perhaps horrify us. Those emotions are as real as they are automatic, and as much as we might wish we felt otherwise, honesty demands that we acknowledge at least to ourselves how we feel. Love, on the other hand, is an act of the will, a decision that, regardless of what emotions we're feeling, commits us to overriding them. It is crucial for children to understand as early as possible the difference between liking and loving—that when we're angry or disappointed with them, that doesn't mean we no longer love them. Most children figure out fairly early that they're not always likable. The knowledge, however, that even when they're not likable they're nevertheless lovable is what ultimately frees them to be themselves. And learning from their experience with their parents that they are not simply subject to their emotions but can actually gain control of them frees them to become adults.

What is so crucial about loving our children no matter what is that if they are to learn such love, it will likely be from us, and if we fail to provide it, they may never learn it at all. That loss seriously undermines not only their sense of security and self-worth but also their capacity to form relationships. People who have never known such love are severely handicapped in their relationships, often willing at best to give only as much as they receive, sometimes even demanding more than they give, and unable to risk the vulnerability that genuine relationships require.

Being parents means conducting our own lives as adults. "Do as I say, not as I do" has never worked very well as a parental directive. No one is better at flushing out our hypocrisy than our children, and it undermines their understanding of what it means to be an adult far more deeply than we imagine. They may use us as examples of how not to behave, but more likely, they will copy us. It's worthwhile to give some thought to the kind of adults we'd like our children to be and then try to model that behavior. (Not the least of the benefits of this approach is that we ourselves may grow up a bit as a result.)

If we were asked, for example, "Do you want your children to grow up to be honest?" virtually all of us would answer, "Yes, of course!" But how often do we compromise on honesty in our own affairs or in our relationships with our children? Looking back, I can't think of a single example in dealing with my children when out-and-out dishonesty would have been justified. You know—those white lies we sometimes tell because, in the moment, it seems easier than the complicated explanation that appears to be the only alternative. Kids have long memories, and they hold us accountable. It may take years, but sooner or later, that little white lie may come back to haunt you. Not only can it throw a monkey wrench into our relationships with our children; it can also compromise their own sense of integrity. "If Dad can play a bit loose with the truth, how honest do I have to be?"

Our kids are always watching us, and that's tough, because none of us is perfect. Honesty, humility, and the willingness to admit our mistakes go a long way toward compensating for our human frailty. Laughing at ourselves—even letting our kids laugh at us—can reap lasting rewards, initially humbling though the experience may be. Most of our children come away from honest encounters less disappointed with our imperfections than relieved of the pressure to be perfect themselves.

Perhaps the most telling sign of our children's comfort in their own skin is their ability to be alone without becoming either lonely or bored. As important as relationship is in our development, no relationship is more important, ultimately, than our relationship with ourselves, yet our extroverted culture doesn't give us much chance to work on that. If circumstances force their children to be physically alone, parents frequently keep them occupied with electronic "friends" like TV or computer games to protect them from boredom. Now, I'm no Luddite; I can no longer imagine life without my laptop, and I rejoice in the invention of the internet and its accessibility to billions around the world—surely as significant a revolution as our era has produced. And it's true that electronic games can be both interactive and educational and can help children develop important skills. But sometimes it may be worthwhile to challenge our children to work their way out of boredom using their own creative resources, if only so that they discover the self-satisfaction of being able to do so.

Our family owns a vacation home in the North Woods of Maine, where there is no TV or wi-fi. Spending a month or two there each summer, our children were forced to use their imaginations, turning boulders into space ships, inventing games, and in general using the environment in creative ways. The remoteness, relative silence, and seemingly endless space encouraged them to spend countless hours on their own, sailing on a sunfish, paddling a kayak, camping on a beach, or just sitting on a rock thinking. I know all of them continue to cherish those solo moments.

"Loner" is a negative epithet in America that conjures images of the likes of Lee Harvey Oswald and Ted Kaczynski. The last thing we want a child to be is a loner, though despite America's reverence for popularity and our cultural preference for extroversion, some of our children are bound to be introverts by nature, and, after all, few introverts turn out to be psychopaths. But whether our children are extroverts or introverts, in our attempts to ensure that they won't be outsiders, we may rob them of the talent for being alone. To help them find equilibrium between solitude and relationship, we have to start when they are toddlers. To be sure, some of us are extroverts and some introverts by nature, but all of us need to become comfortable with ourselves, and all of us require from earliest childhood some time alone to make sense of what life throws at us.

In *The Call of Solitude,* psychologist Esther Buchholz observes, "We live in a society that worships independence yet deeply fears alienation: our era is sped-up and overconnected…. Life's creative solutions require alonetime. Solitude is required for the unconscious to process and unravel problems. Others inspire us, information feeds us, practice improves our performance, but we need quiet time to figure things out, to emerge with new discoveries, to unearth original answers."[36]

Our son Taylor had an early passion for Legos which persists even today. (When he was a junior in college, we gave him for Christmas a Lego model of Falling Water, Frank Lloyd Wright's masterpiece, which he immediately completed and subsequently displayed proudly in his dorm room.) As a small child, he played happily for hours, using his imagination to create whole narratives around his constructions and solving design problems in an off-beat manner that became his hallmark. Taylor's Lego buildings were never symmetrical window-door-window buildings. Instead, he favored more abstract, cantilevered designs that gave visual and concrete expression to his characteristically out-of-the-box thinking. Solo play gave him ample opportunity to take up problems, work through solutions, and stick with a project until he thought he was done. Taylor is no loner; to the contrary, he's an extrovert with strong intuitive people skills, honed, in no small measure, by the time he spends alone getting a better understanding of himself. He has close and loyal friends, and he *is* a close and loyal friend. But there aren't many people his age who could or would have taken a two-week solo hike in the Adirondacks, as he did the summer before his senior year of college.

You don't have live on Walden Pond to develop a talent for solitude. Solo time requires no more than a room where you can close the door, or a place to take a walk, even in a busy city. The key is to provide a sufficient stimulus to elicit emotional response and productive thought but not so much as to overwhelm. Headphones, as alienating as they can sometimes be, do seem to help some people find solitude in an otherwise crowded existence. A journal can assist with focus. Our daughter Hilary has been journaling regularly since third grade, finding it a useful outlet for her emotions and an effective way to gain perspective on her life. The goal is to create a space and time in which one can just *think*.

If you count the number of times while reading this that you've stopped to answer the phone, respond to a text, or read your email, you will have just a sliver of the sense of what makes it so hard for the millennial generation to find space and time to think. Our electronic devices are becoming increasingly cybernetic—iPhones 'R Us. The younger you are, the more likely this is true of you. The benefits are manifold, of course. Our opportunities to explore the universe seem boundless. Moreover, the far-ranging accessibility of technology even to people off the grid, thanks to satellites, and its adherence to a matrix rather than a hierarchical structure make the information revolution of the late 20th and early 21st centuries the most democratic in history. But it is also the most ubiquitous, and unless we actively protect them, it will render both privacy and sacred space relics of the past.

Since everybody and his brother-in-law are writing these days about the loss of privacy, I won't add much here. Suffice it to say that we are raising a generation with serious boundary issues, willing to spill their innards on Facebook and then outraged that, thanks to their "friends," their innards have gone viral. Like any new technology, social media such as Facebook have quickly outpaced the development of reasonable norms for their use, and the norms will presumably catch up—but only if everyone remains aware of what is at risk, like privacy, confidentiality, reputation, the true definition of "friends," social boundaries, and the ability politely but firmly to say "No." And all of that doesn't even begin to deal with security.

By "sacred space," I'm not just talking about churches, mosques, and synagogues; I'm thinking, as well, of Central Park, or Grand Canyon, or Mt. Katahdin, where serene moments are so often interrupted these days by a ringing cell phone. Sacred time is an issue, as well. If we are available for calls, email, and texts throughout the day (and night?), when is down time? When do we get a chance to think without interruption? If we are to be successful in encouraging reflection in our young people, we need to give them strategies for structuring their time as well as their use of technology. There's no way to force them to do it, of course. But if they come to appreciate the benefits of uninterrupted silence, perhaps they will be convinced.

Unfortunately, of course, not everyone is comfortable with silence, and many in the generation raised on fast-image TV and video games have become hooked on the adrenalin rush, becoming easily bored without external stimulation. Awakening the ability to be entertained by low-stimulus activities like reading or bird-watching may be more challenging today than in previous generations, but there is no less need among today's young people—indeed among their elders, as well—to learn the art of simply being, as opposed to constantly doing, or, as is more often the case with our electronic appendages, being constantly done unto.

No matter how thoughtful and reflective our children are, though, most of them need guidance to help them appropriately integrate all of the pieces of our world. Parents and teachers play that role to some extent, but many American teenagers are abandoned to one another for the kind of advice once provided by a godparent, a grandparent, a member of the clergy, a coach, a scout leader, a camp counselor, an employer, a favorite aunt or uncle, a neighbor, or a friend's parent—some adult other than a parent who served as a role model and a presence in a teen's life. Adolescence is a period when teens need to break from their parents in order to establish their own identities, but they aren't ready to do without adults altogether.

When I preach at baptisms, I generally surprise godparents with the following admonition: "Your job is not to make sure this infant becomes a good Episcopalian. We really have no way of knowing whether that's what God has in mind for her. Your job is to love her unconditionally, doing everything you can to let her know you support her in becoming whomever God intends her to be. You're at least one adult to whom she should be able to turn when she'd rather not turn to her parents for advice, and that means building a relationship of trust from this point onward."

I'm sure some would brand me a heretic for suggesting that keeping their godchildren in the Christian fold is not godparents' first responsibility. As a religious convert myself, though, who am I to discourage a young person from following a divinely led path, even if it isn't mine? What our young people need most are adults willing to guide them as they explore, letting them take the lead, rather than telling them where they should end up and how to get there.

Our children are growing up without such mentors, however. Families are so scattered geographically that many children barely know their grandparents and rarely see their aunts and uncles. While the Gallup Poll has estimated American weekly religious observance at 40% for some time, other researchers have questioned that statistic, finding that those polled often dissemble about such things. Checking the statistics against actual church attendance, Religioustolerance.org arrives at a figure closer to 20%, and other pollsters have backed the smaller figure. [37] Since worship remains one of the few intergenerational activities in American life, the decline in church attendance to 1 in 5 suggests that as many as 80% of our children may rarely be exposed to adults other than their parents and teachers. Increasingly, we are segregated residentially by age, with many seniors residing in communities where children are not even permitted to live. Other than teachers, there are virtually no adults in most children's lives who relate to them as whole people—and regrettably few teachers have such relationships with their students. Where are they to turn when they begin to wrestle with questions without easy solutions? We've left them little choice: they turn to each other. And while they sometimes give each other surprisingly good advice, at least as often the blind are leading the blind.

One of the problems is the persistence of the spurious myth of the nuclear family—a unit comprising two parents, 2.3 children, a dog, a house, and a (full) two-car garage. The house has a wall or fence around it, and the family is entirely self-sufficient. The only problem is that no such family exists, although this image is an icon of American life. Quite apart from the fact that, according to the 2000 census, roughly 30% of American children are living in single-parent families,[38] even those families that include two biological parents have needs that they themselves cannot meet. The weakness of the extended family in modern America has resulted in substantial hardship and even crisis for many of our fellow citizens. There are few natural communities of trust, people with whom we have developed close relationships when times are good so that they are there for us when we are in need.

Extended families need not be related by blood—they can be families in the neighborhood, people with whom we socialize, people whose interests and values we share. At their best, religious communities are extended families. It is through extended families that our children develop close relationships with adults other than their parents and begin to decide for themselves whom they can depend on. It is with those people that they begin to learn the talent of being with adults, the skills to converse with them, and the wherewithal to develop their own relationships with adults even outside the extended family. If our children are to have meaningful mentors, then we have to make it a priority to place in their path people we believe have the capacity to play that role for them, and we must encourage those relationships from the time our children are born.

Exposing our children to communities of trust—church youth groups, bible studies, campus ministries, scout troops, outdoor adventure groups, clubs or activities organized around common interests—helps them recognize their need for such communities and encourages them to seek them on their own initiative. Giving them opportunities to become civically involved, to do community service, or to become involved in causes they care about helps them establish a set of values in the context of the larger world in which they live. Welcoming their participation in causes we care about can give them the valuable experience of working alongside their parents, and while they may not replicate our passion for the cause, the exposure to the commitment of others can be a powerful inspiration for them to seek causes they believe in.

If the most important role of parents is to love their children unconditionally, surely the most difficult is love's most challenging demand: letting them go. It sounds like a contradiction—holding them tight and letting them go—but that is the essence of unconditional love. Most of us are control freaks, and our difficulty in letting go of our children is born of our fear that we'll lose control of what they become—control we come to learn at some point we never really had in the first place. Loving our children must ultimately include the trust that they can and indeed must take charge of their own destinies along with the humility to acknowledge that whatever vision we may have for them is our vision, not theirs. The reality is that they can't become adults without separating from us, and we can either fight that process or bless it.

Of course, our children generally begin the process of separating from us well before we believe they're ready, and the safety net of other adults whom both they and we trust can help parents let go. Sometimes events occur beyond anyone's control that, on the one hand, reinforce the limits of our power and, on the other, make us want to hang on for dear life to what little control we do have.

Our daughter Hilary had a stroke half a block from our house the day before her 15th birthday as a result of a clotting disorder she inherited from me. It was by far the most harrowing experience my wife and I have ever been through. She was initially paralyzed on the right side and both her speech and cognitive processing were severely compromised. As we all celebrated her fifteenth birthday in intensive care, we weren't yet sure she would survive let alone ever return to school. In just five weeks, though, she regained most of what she had lost, returned to school on time in September, and three years later, was accepted early at Bowdoin College. No one would wish a stroke on a teenager, but I have to confess that Hilary's recovery showed her and the rest of us grit none of us knew she had, and she herself would admit that some of her best qualities—her compassion, her determination, her resilience, and her commitment to those with challenges—are closely related to her recovery from the stroke.

During the winter following her stroke, Hilary expressed eagerness to join her brother the following summer on a wilderness trip in the Rockies sponsored by his summer camp. They would be camping for a couple of weeks, and though emergency assistance would be available, they would be in true wilderness. In addition, the hiking and rock climbing would be physically daunting. We were frankly impressed that she wanted to do it, as she had not formerly been drawn to such activities. Clearly, she was eager to prove she could do it. As much as we wanted to encourage her, we were nevertheless somewhat nervous about the idea. After all, we'd nearly lost her. Was it responsible so soon to send her off on such a challenging trip? But as my wife observed, the worst thing that had ever happened to any of our children had taken place within sight of our front door, and we had been powerless to prevent it. We knew we had to let her go on the trip, even aware as we were of the dangers. That life itself is dangerous is a fact worth acknowledging when we bring children into the world. Protecting them from unnecessary danger is certainly our responsibility as parents, but keeping them from testing themselves in reasonable and well-supervised ways stunts their growth. The image of Hilary on the cover of the following year's brochure smiling ear-to-ear as she scaled a vertical cliff says it all, though, of course, few people who saw that photograph knew she had been paralyzed and fighting for her life just a year earlier.

Nothing brings home the difficulty of letting go more dramatically, however, than when our children get themselves into trouble. We see them in pain, and we want to save them from it. Letting go doesn't mean turning our backs on our children, but it does sometimes mean letting them fail, insisting on their accepting the consequences of their acts, standing beside them as they do, and helping them fully understand what has happened. It also means remembering it's not about us.

In November of his senior year in college, our son Justin hit a stone wall. Initially, he hid the problem from my wife Carrie and me, but gradually we became aware that something was seriously wrong. At last, he called me, having learned from his girlfriend (now his wife) that we knew enough to be worried. I could hear that he was in tears as he said to me, "Dad, I'm really in trouble." In the seconds of silence that followed that remark, I imagined all the things he might have done, so that when he laid it all out, I was actually deeply relieved. "My grade-point has fallen below 3.0, so I'm out of the practice teaching program. I have four papers due next week, and there's no way I can get it all done. I'm in way over my head." It wasn't just my relief that he hadn't killed someone or burned down the dorm that led me to respond, "Justin, I know it's hard for you to imagine this right now, because you're feeling completely up against it, but you're going to be ok. I wish I were there to help you believe that. Do you want me to come up?" "Dad!," he responded, the frustration obvious in his voice, "did you hear anything I just said? There's no point in your coming up—you can't write my papers."

A bit of background. Justin has ADHD, is very bright, and up to and obviously including this incident, had always pushed deadlines right to the edge, but he had always somehow been able to pull the rabbit out of the hat. Carrie and I had said to each other many times, "When do you suppose he's going to crash?" I assumed as I held the phone that the moment had come.

"I heard every word," I responded. "Justin, I deal daily with people in their 40's and 50's who are where you are. The difference is, they lose their marriages, their families, their jobs, and their fortunes. What's the worst thing that could happen to you?"

He shot back, "Dad, I may not graduate from Bowdoin." "You'll graduate," I said, with, I confess, more confidence than I felt. "You may not graduate on time, but you'll graduate—and maybe with a better education as a result of all of this. Will the sun continue to rise and set?" There was a long pause as he absorbed what I was saying and understood for the first time that he was probably going to survive this crisis—or, at least, that his father seemed certain he would. "Dad," he said hesitantly, "I think I'd like you to come up."

I did fly up to Bowdoin that afternoon. At Justin's request, I accompanied him to the Dean's office, where Justin and the Dean mapped out a plan that might enable my son to climb out of the hole he'd dug for himself. He was right, of course—I couldn't write his papers for him, nor did I have any interest in doing so. My role was cheerleader; he had to carry the ball. Justin stuck to the plan and, in fact, managed to graduate on time. But more important, the experience taught him that he could win a fight against pretty serious odds. And it taught him something else, too. He came to realize that this crisis had been no accident. He had been headed for teaching, but his ADHD made him claustrophobic in the classroom, a problem of which he was still largely unconscious. It ultimately became clear to him that he had sabotaged himself in order to keep from going into a career that would have been extremely stressful for him.

Justin now administers a program that helps disadvantaged kids get into college, graduate, and become employed, and I know his own brush with failure at Bowdoin has made him a more effective counselor as he helps young people bounce back from crises that mirror his own. He'll be a better parent, as well.

Children *will* fail. Parents can't prevent them from doing so. Pretending the failure didn't happen, moving the goal posts, blaming someone else, or any of the thousand other ways parents have of helping their children avoid failure simply puts off the evil day. Children who are permitted to fail suffer pain and loss, to be sure. But those whose parents protect them from failure live in perpetual fear of it; they know that, sooner or later, their imperfections will catch up with them. Learning that few people die of failure and that, indeed, failure is one of the principal ingredients of lasting success is what gives us resilience in the face of life's trials.

Let me return to that moment when I asked Justin, in the midst of his meltdown, if he wanted me to come up to Bowdoin. It's reasonable to ask if I was being a "helicopter parent." Wouldn't it have been better simply to call a dean, or his adviser, and let one of them handle it? My judgment came down to two observations: 1) this is no ordinary meltdown—he's close to crashing; and 2) part of what he's upset about is letting his parents down; we need to let him know both that we're not the issue and that we love him, warts and all, and there may be no more effective way to do that than to be there. It wasn't an easy call, and in the end, I went with my gut—but my gut is by no means always right.

A college dean with whom I recently discussed this book asked rhetorically, "When do they leave the nest these days?" It's a fair question. A surprising number of students have nearly daily contact with their parents. There needs to come a point when the relationship between parents and their children moves from parent-to-child to adult-to-adult. If our kids never leave, how does that transformation happen? They need time on their own to demonstrate to their parents and themselves that they can stand on their own two feet and manage their lives. Of course, most parents have little confidence that their children can manage their way out of a paper bag, and while that observation may be partially true, it results in large part because parents don't always get to see their children at their best. But if parents don't give children room to fail, they won't have room to grow. And children who never achieve adult-to-adult relationships with their parents are often hard-pressed to be adults with anyone else.

I had already written that paragraph when our youngest, a recent graduate of Skidmore College, put my resolve to the test. The summer camp that employed him the summer after graduation and where he had spent thirteen previous summers offered him a job in their winter program, a leadership school for teenagers. In the current economic climate, that offer looked pretty good to Carrie and me. It was a known quantity, a solid institution, and—most important—included health insurance. But though initially interested, Taylor finally turned it down. His real interest was younger children. He'd spent too much of his childhood at the camp to be able to feel entirely like an adult there. And as big as the State of Maine is and as much as he loves us, he felt compelled to start out on his own. So he packed all of his worldly goods into his car and took off for Boulder, Colorado, accurately observing, "I know I don't have a place to live or a job, but I'm not going to find either from here."

And off he went. My principal worry, frankly, was the health insurance. As I'm on Medicare, he couldn't join my policy, and though COBRA allowed him to continue his Skidmore medical insurance, that would run out in February. I don't think either of us thought Taylor would end up jobless and homeless—he did have savings and plenty of contacts in Boulder. But the state of the economy gave us no confidence that he'd find anything soon. Would he end up spinning his wheels and become demoralized or, worse, depressed?

I wrote him a letter, a sufficient rarity between us to give it some impact. I began by letting him know his mom and I were behind him as he set off on his own—that we believed in him and blessed his journey. And then, without undermining his persistent optimism that this was all going to work, I urged him to be sure to maintain his principal goal—working with kids. If the job didn't come through, he could always find volunteer work with kids. Not ideal, perhaps, but as work with kids is what turns him on and keeps him going, that, it seemed to me, was the priority. I closed by being a dad:

> Call us once a week. You know we'll worry if we don't hear from you, and while we can email and text, it's not the same. We want to hear your voice, know what you're up to and how you're feeling. You may be an adult, but you're still our kid. Besides, we want in on the adventure!

Of course, within a month, Taylor had not just a job but the very one he was looking for, teaching toddlers. His apartment overlooks the Flatirons, which he happily climbs on weekends when he isn't skiing. He's never sounded happier. It might not have worked out so well, of course, but I believe he'd have had the resources to weather the challenges—and so would we. Most important, he did it all on his own terms.

There are other reasons besides legitimate parental concern for parents to hang onto their children. Sometimes it's to try to shape their children in their own image. Parents may be tempted to believe that, as long as their own values are clear and they are themselves good role models, their children's integrity will follow naturally. It doesn't work that way. No matter how much children love and respect their parents, they will not and should not be their parents' carbon copies. As significant as parental influence is, children are influenced in a multitude of ways, and growing up is in no small part about sorting all of that out.

As a university chaplain, I used to say often that my job was to lead young people out of their parents' faith and into their own. Of course, parents who sent what they viewed as devout, life-long Episcopalians to Princeton were sometimes disgruntled by my characterization of a chaplain's role, but the most pressing responsibility of people in their late teens and early twenties is to establish their own terms of identity, to ascertain what it is they believe in, not because their parents do, or because their friends do, or because it's always been that way, but because it is what to them is most apparently true. Young people aren't just influenced from without; they also carry within themselves some level of moral consciousness, and the sorting process about which I'm talking here involves aligning what's coming in from outside with what is part of one's inherent character. Sometimes it is necessary to break down the rigidity of old appropriated ideas in order to make room for the truths inside to emerge.

I recall, for example, a conversation years ago with a young woman who had been part of a parish youth group I led. Her family was evangelically oriented, and her parents and I had had some long and sometimes difficult discussions about whether Christianity is the exclusive route to salvation. They objected to my teaching and preaching that, Christian or not, "we see through a glass darkly"—that none of us has the whole truth, and that it may well be that what we assume to be differences among faiths aren't always as different as they appear. They felt I was taking liberties with the Gospel—but that's a discussion for another book.

The daughter, somewhat conflicted, nevertheless continued during high school to reflect her parents' theology. Then she went to college. When I saw her during her first spring break and asked how she was doing, she was equivocal. She enjoyed college, she said, but she'd left the church. "Really?" I asked. "Why?" She replied, "My roommate is a Buddhist. She's a wonderful girl, more faithful than I ever was. I can't figure out why she and her family should be going to hell just because they're Buddhists." "Neither can I," I responded. And we looked at each other for some time without speaking. A final embrace was our last encounter. I don't know where her spiritual journey has led, but I am reasonably sure the opening of her mind, while painful, ultimately led her closer to her own faith.

It's tough as a parent to make room for your children to believe things you don't. There's certainly nothing wrong with using the art of persuasion, but giving young people the opportunity to do the same lets them know you're willing to respect them even when you don't agree with them. That exercise helps them test their beliefs, and while it is tempting to try to help them avoid all the dead ends and detours you suffered, there aren't really any shortcuts to wisdom.

We need to instill in our children a sense of their own value—value they have by virtue of being human—as well as the responsibility to share that value with the people and the world around them. We need to prepare them to survive failure, disappointment, hardship, and even injustice. We need to help them over their misplaced trust in the Fairness Doctrine. We need to hold them accountable for what they do and don't do. And we need to help them believe sufficiently in themselves and their futures to know that whatever happens, they'll most likely get through it. Parents are in most cases the most important sources of the faith that enables children to avoid the trap of victimhood and get past even the most daunting of obstacles. The earliest thing I can remember my own parents saying, and they said it every time the world failed to go my way, was, "Pick it up, dust it off, and use it over again." Not bad advice.

Within the space of a week-and-a-half recently, my wife and I watched our youngest graduate from college, our oldest get married, and our middle child turn 25. It was one of those whirlwind times when you know what you're going through is momentous but you don't have time to process it all. Only when the actual events were all behind us did Carrie look at me and say, "I think we've done it." Exactly what we've done may not ever be clear. We certainly haven't finished being parents. They still look to us for advice and support, an occasional meal, and a sympathetic ear. The gratifying commitment they all have to family means they're in touch with us and one another pretty regularly. But our distance from the decision-making in their lives is something for which both they and we are ready. I'd like to think that means we raised them right, but what it may actually mean is that they raised us right. Of course, Yogi would remind us all that it ain't over till it's over.

CHAPTER 11

Educating for Adulthood

Clearly, we depend on schools to help prepare our children to be adults, and yet, ironically, American education's ubiquitous emphasis on preparation may be its biggest liability as a molder of maturity. From kindergarten on, it seems, far more attention is paid to where children are going than to where they are. We are pleased to see them achieve milestones, but primarily because those achievements indicate they're on track to meet objectives down the road. Reading early may mean they're brighter than their peers, which may mean they'll excel in primary school, which may mean they'll get into a selective secondary school, which may mean they'll get into Harvard. Why not just be excited that now that they can read, a whole new universe of knowledge and pleasure is accessible to them?

Our nearly universal understanding of education as a means to an end rather than an end in itself undervalues both education and the learner. We lament, for example, that "nobody knows any history anymore." Yet we teach history not so much as something to *know*—i.e., to integrate into our being—as a body of facts to remember long enough to be able to check the right boxes on a standardized test when it's time to demonstrate proficiency. Since a real understanding of history requires not just the memorization of a laundry list of facts (which few will hold onto for very long in any case) but the ability to relate those facts into trends and ideas and to draw inferences from what one learns of human behavior over time, it's hardly surprising that not many young people these days know much history. It is especially unfortunate that our best students get some of the worst teaching: AP American History moves so quickly ("We need to finish it all before the AP test in May") as to make virtually impossible the kind of intellectual exploration that might promote real enjoyment of history. Similarly, in math, all that seems important is how quickly students can go. Understanding why they're doing what they're doing takes a back seat to their being able simply to do it. I got A's in math, but I didn't understand that trigonometry was about ratios until well after I took it; and though I achieved two years' worth of A's in both high school and college calculus, all I really know about it is that it has something to do with the rate of change. That seems a pretty shoddy return on the investment.

In its future orientation, our system values proficiency over understanding. The question every student is taught to ask is, "Where will this get me?" Ultimately, we even gloss proficiency with diplomas and degrees that are meant to indicate proficiency but often simply mask incompetence. Is it any wonder that so many American college students are simply in it for the degree? We've told them they need a college degree to get a decent job. We haven't told them they need to know anything. As the authors of *Academically Adrift* note with more than a little alarm, all too many college students party their way through school, doing the minimum work necessary to get the degree, which they obtain with great éclat, only to discover to their own dismay that it turns out they were supposed to learn something along the way.

Fortunately, a great many students—the majority, it would appear—are not so profligate with their time in college. And some actually find in college a chance to investigate areas of knowledge just for the joy of doing so. Liberal arts colleges pride themselves on encouraging just such pursuits, but increasingly, those colleges find they are speaking a different language from the one students have heard in school until then. "Where's it going to get me?" isn't a question for which study for its own sake has an answer.

What does all of this have to do with growing up? Maturity of mind may not be all there is to being an adult; maturity of character may be more to the point. But I would argue that mature character requires a mature mind, and that there's no necessary connection between maturity of mind and 800's on the SAT's or 5's on the AP exams, let alone a college degree. Maturity of mind has to do with the capacity for creative reflection, for drawing reasonable inferences about the information and ideas one receives, for self-understanding, for finding one's place in the world, for perceiving the world from the point of view of others, for admitting error. Maturity of mind is the ability at once to achieve consistency of thought and to let go of that consistency when it fails you. The mature mind is able to hold conflicting ideas without coming apart and is unthreatened by ambiguity. The mature mind fervently seeks the truth but is able to be wrong—indeed, interprets error as a pathway toward the truth. What if the No Child Left Behind Act judged schools according to their students' success in meeting those criteria?

The federal requirement to teach to content tests makes it difficult for teachers to give sufficient attention to *how* children think; they're too busy ensuring that *what* they think conforms to state testing requirements. But focus on how they think is crucial if we are to have any success at getting them to think like adults.

How, for example, do we prepare them to be citizens? Yes, they need information about the way American government works, they need a working knowledge of the Constitution, and they need to understand the privileges and responsibilities of citizenship. But they surely get, at best, a mixed message when such subjects are taught, as they often are, in contexts that are thoroughly undemocratic, in which students are given little voice and less authority. They understand the meaning and consequences of democratic process far better in classrooms that replicate, at least to some extent, the system they are studying, where they don't just memorize a definition of democracy but actually experience it. It's one thing to read about the Lincoln-Douglas debates. But when all students are required to be Lincoln or Douglas and stand at the podium, they are forced to think about the issues in ways that grow their minds, not just their information banks. Participating in arguments with classmates about states' rights is likely to provide a far deeper understanding not only of the nuances of the issue but also of the ambiguity about who is right. Such experiences, indeed, can change the way students think about and deal with conflict.

The pendulum swings in education between content and process, as though one without the other were even conceivable; I am by no means pleading for content-free education, whatever that would be. But the magic bullet of testing has so concentrated the educational establishment on content that sheer quantity of information can easily overwhelm attention to the way minds interact in the classroom. And as much as maturity may depend on possession of a body of knowledge, it depends at least as much on the ways we think about what we know.

To the extent that students can become their own teachers, they begin to discover that teaching and learning are not as opposite as they often appear, with one person occupying the role of teacher and another, the role of student. Good teachers are constantly learning from their students, and teachers who acknowledge as much enhance the learning process for students, who begin to understand that they have a responsibility in the process not simply to be passive receivers. Teachers can encourage students in groups to teach one another. While being receivers can make us feel infantilized, nothing empowers us more than to become givers, and teachers have the power to challenge their students to be both receivers and givers and offer them, thereby, a taste of adulthood—which is not meant to suggest that there's no room in education for the old-fashioned lecture. As one accustomed to "lecturing" weekly from the pulpit, I could hardly defend such a position. But the mark of a good lecture (or sermon, for that matter) is a level of engagement that beckons the active—albeit silent—participation of the listeners. The stimulating lecturer excites our imaginations, drawing out thoughts we may not have known we had, leading us to integrate some of the lecturer's thoughts with our own and run with them. We get excited about some lecturers and preachers less, I think, because of their independent wisdom and insight than because of their capacity to engage us—to send us off lecturing or preaching to ourselves.

Whenever we can break down the boundary between students and teachers, it is worth considering. Promoting a sense of collegiality between students and teachers without sacrificing whatever decorum the circumstances demand helps students exercise some of their adult muscles. I was on the faculty at a school that used the time between terms to run short week-long courses taught by the faculty, who were encouraged to choose subjects they cared about but in which they didn't need to be experts. I taught a course on the architecture of what was then the new Boston City Hall. My students, who were in these mini-courses entirely by choice, all shared my interest in architecture; in fact, a few knew at least as much as I did. The chance to explore new territory together changed our relationships and gave many of those students confidence in that venue that they had not shown in their standard courses. Long after the short course was over, most of those students and I continued to relate on the adult plane we had established while exploring 20th century architecture together. In the 35 years that have followed, probably few if any of us have found any practical application for what we learned that week about the architecture of Boston City Hall, but I would confidently wager that all of us recall the experience as significant.

I've watched my son Taylor establish a tone of collegiality with the pre-school children with whom he has worked, and he's been a successful camp counselor in large part because of the sense of partnership he's able to achieve between himself and his 12-year-old campers. It's not a pretense of equality; it's simple respect, and it can be established with children of any age. The older they are, though, the more important that respect is, not only because it communicates an expectation of increasing maturity, but also because it serves as a model for their behavior in relationships, and it's a way of subtly encouraging them to take increased responsibility for their education.

At the post-secondary level, such collegiality ought to be the norm and often is, especially in academic settings where students and faculty have high expectations of one another. Examples abound of student-faculty research collaboration, creative student independent work, and seminars requiring substantial student leadership. Of course, collegiality is difficult to maintain if students and faculty aren't on the same page with respect to the standard of work expected, though in such cases, some faculty are successful at drawing their students into more mature behavior, while others simply fall into a more parental role. Treating students as adults even when they act like children isn't easy, but it may be the best way to hold them accountable.

If the failure of a sizable bloc of America's undergraduates to engage academically is vexing, what has college deans and presidents really tearing their hair out is alcohol. It's not a new problem, of course. Drunkenness among college students has likely existed for as long as there have been college students. But the intensity of abuse and the extremity of the consequences make drinking on campus today an exponentially more serious problem than it was a generation or two ago. According to statistics from the National Institute on Alcohol Abuse and Alcoholism, excessive drinking, which affects virtually every college campus in America, resulted in 1999 in 1825 deaths of college students; 599,000 injuries; 696,000 assaults; and 97,000 incidents of sexual assault or acquaintance rape (a crime, as observed earlier, that is substantially under-reported). 11% of all students in 2009 reported having committed an act of vandalism while under the influence of alcohol.[39] And in a 2005 Harvard School of Public Health study that surveyed more than 14,000 students at 119 4-year institutions, 31% acknowledged symptoms that classified them as abusive drinkers.[40] What these statistics can't measure is the toll alcohol takes on the general tone of campus life, personal relationships, and individual emotional development.

Of course, one of the problems with alcohol in American society is that the legal right to drink has always been one of the prominent milestones of growing up, along with getting a driver's license, voting, and becoming eligible to join the military. That one can be sent off to die at 18 but can't buy a drink until turning 21 is simply not possible to justify rationally but a product of the patchwork of sometimes inconsistent social legislation crafted by lobbying forces pitted against one another in the halls of Congress. With good reason, Mothers Against Drunk Driving has succeeded in getting the driving age raised in most states, but the result is that many young people start driving at the same time they go off to college, where alcohol abuse is epidemic. A generation of inexperienced drivers with no parental supervision in an alcohol-soaked environment is surely not what MADD intended; but that's what the law has created.

Let's face it—no one has a silver bullet for this one. In 2008, John McCardell, former president of Middlebury College, started the Amethyst Initiative, joined by 130 college presidents seeking to lower the drinking age to 18.[41] Arguing that current law is bad social policy, as widely ignored on college campuses as Prohibition was across America, these college leaders sought a return to the brief period between 1974 and 1987 when an 18-year-old could legally purchase a beer, when college administrators didn't find themselves in the present uncomfortable no-man's land between their students and law enforcement agencies, and when faculty and students could enjoy a friendly beer together at the campus pub. In the current political climate, however, this initiative doesn't stand a ghost of a chance.

So what's the answer? Making alcohol the target has had limited success; it is quite simply too deeply embedded in American culture. To be sure, campuses have no choice but to set clear limits, to establish party guidelines, to cooperate with local law enforcement agents in enforcing the law, and to take appropriate action against students who violate campus regulations. But no dean wants the role of police officer; people don't become deans of academic institutions to spend all of their time enforcing rules, surveying damage, and picking up bodies.

The solution may lie, however, in the true mission of undergraduate institutions: instead of targeting alcohol, perhaps schools should go back to targeting students and education. It's time for schools to help students redefine their academic and social life so that they cease to see them as diametrically opposed. Even at America's finest universities and among our brightest students, the acknowledged culture is to work hard and play hard—and play hard they do. But what that culture overlooks is the possibility of integrating work and play, and I would argue that the integration of work and play should be the first order of business of post-secondary institutions, especially residential institutions, which are best situated to accomplish it.

On most campuses, class schedules are heaviest from Monday through Thursday. Fridays tend to be light, and a great many faculty and students do what they can to avoid Friday classes. The result is that partying begins Thursday night, and from Thursday night until Monday morning, campuses become adolescent universes, in which the oldest person around is 22. If one were to try to construct an environment whose purpose is to bring out the absolute worst in students, one couldn't do a better job.

I spent eleven years working at one of the world's premier universities. Princeton accepts only 8% of its applicants, and even most of those who aren't accepted are themselves a pretty stellar group. They've led nonprofit initiatives, written books, made scientific discoveries, scaled Everest, performed at Carnegie Hall, and led their peers in every conceivable way. These are some of the most accomplished young people on the planet, and the maturity that comes through in their applications is pretty impressive.

Yet when these same people arrive on campus and get into the spirit of a party weekend, a substantial number of them go haywire.

What if campus life were arranged differently, so that not only work and play but also the older and younger members of the community engaged with one another seven days a week?

Of course, the first question any college administrator is bound to ask is, "Would anybody come?" A fair question. Are there faculty around who are prepared to be involved on weekends? And are there students around who are prepared to welcome faculty into their social lives? Perhaps the more accurate question is, are there faculty and students who might be interested in a radical transformation of the way education and social life happen on campus?

The answer is at least a qualified yes. There isn't a lot of radical transformation going on at the collegiate level, but there is at least some change at the margins. And a few places have in fact taken some giant steps out of the mainstream that may provide compelling models.

Small residential liberal arts colleges have long prided themselves on their level of student-faculty interaction. Why would a first-rate biochemist teach at a place like tiny Bowdoin College in Brunswick, Maine, where there are no graduate students, no medical school, no major metropolitan area, and not many other biochemists? Only because he or she is committed to teaching undergraduates. Bowdoin manages to attract a premier faculty full of leaders in their fields, but they are all people for whom teaching is a priority. If it weren't, they'd surely go elsewhere, as virtually all of them could. Many Bowdoin faculty members take an active interest in the lives of their students, and it is certainly not uncommon to spot faculty on the sidelines of a lacrosse game or in the audience of a student concert. But faculty members don't live on campus, and they tend to clear out on weekends, which for many include Friday (only 10% of Bowdoin's classes happen on Fridays).[42] As a result, like almost every other college in America, Bowdoin is one place from Monday morning through Thursday afternoon and quite another from Thursday evening to Monday morning. For fully 46% of the week, then, there are relatively few student-faculty interactions—certainly a lot fewer than during the other half of the week. As long as that situation persists, as it does nearly everywhere, it's hard to imagine how colleges will achieve a meaningful integration of intellectual and social life, no matter how bright their students are—and Bowdoin's students are at the top of the heap.

There are some ways of manipulating campus life that can produce at least subtle changes in campus tone. Skidmore College, which is only slightly larger than Bowdoin and slightly less selective but otherwise similar, has taken a small but effective step toward making social life at least a bit more intellectual. First-year students, each of whom must enroll in one of a large variety of semester-long seminars on topics of general interest, are given rooming assignments according to their seminar choices. The results are at least two-fold: their roommates as well as those living down the hall are likely to share some of their intellectual interests; and the conversations that go on in the seminars are likely to flow over into the dormitories. Whether there is any long-term effect is difficult to measure, but as a visitor to the campus when my son was a student there, I was surprised at how often I overheard spirited scholarly conversation among students sitting casually on the quad. Skidmore's motto is, "Creative Thought Matters," a motto that drives much of what the College does and no doubt attracts an intellectually curious student body, but I am inclined to give the first-year rooming arrangement at least some of the credit. Still, however, Skidmore's weekend situation isn't marginally different from Bowdoin's.

More than 100 years ago, as president of Princeton, Woodrow Wilson seems to have had the issue of educating for adulthood very much on his mind as he imagined a university where graduate students, undergraduates, and faculty would live and work together as a community of scholars.[43] He envisioned much of the intellectual activity of the University happening in the residence halls, which he referred to as "colleges," as they are called at Oxford and Cambridge, Wilson's models. In fact, generations before Princeton would finally be persuaded by its wisdom, both Yale and Harvard adopted Wilson's College Plan (Harvard refers to its residential colleges as "houses"), which Princeton has spent the last century backing into. It took 65 years for Wilson's own university even to begin to institute his proposal, and even then, residential colleges were only for first- and second-year students. It wasn't until 2007 that Princeton finally began to realize Wilson's full vision with the establishment of its first 4-year residential college. As of 2011, three of the six residential colleges include all four classes as well as faculty and graduate students; little by little, they're getting there.

The problem at all three institutions, however, is that neither the houses at Harvard nor the colleges at Yale and Princeton have ever really controlled the social life on campus, which continues to be unduly influenced by socially exclusive organizations like secret societies, selective eating clubs, and fraternities and sororities which, though they directly serve a minority of students at each school, nevertheless retain outsized social power. Such organizations fragment their campuses, shredding rather than knitting together the social fabric and, however subtly, undermining by the very nature of their exclusivity the institution's mission to expand rather than close its students' minds. While they continue to thrive, Woodrow Wilson's dream of a community of scholars—and with it, their increased maturity of mind—is likely to take a back seat.

What's the answer, then? How do we reinvent college—which takes at least four of the most important years of young people's lives as well as not a little of their cash—so that it ceases to be a haven for adolescence and instead more actively nurtures in students the willingness to relinquish adolescence in favor of lives of intention and purpose?

In a valley near Asheville, North Carolina, whose lushness belies the widespread poverty of Appalachia, sits Warren Wilson College, a small liberal arts college that grew out of a Presbyterian mission school.[44] What sets Warren Wilson apart is its distinctive "Triad" program, which gives equal priority to academics, campus work, and service to a broader community with substantial need. The academic program is pretty much like that at most small liberal arts colleges, with the exceptions of its emphasis on learning by doing and its overt encouragement of collegiality of faculty and students, fostered by the school's generally egalitarian ethos. The 48 majors are a rich offering for its 938 students. But in addition to their academic work, students must work at least 15 hours a week on campus, cleaning bathrooms, pruning trees, feeding the pigs on the campus farm, or any of a hundred other possibilities. With just a skeletal professional maintenance staff, Warren Wilson depends largely on its students to operate and maintain the campus infrastructure. Beyond their campus work requirement, students must complete a total of 100 hours of community service by the time they graduate, choosing from an abundant and diverse set of options.

Most schools offer plenty of service opportunities and point with pride to the fact that their service programs are the most popular activity on campus. But while a solid percentage of students participate minimally (perhaps once or twice a year), a much smaller number participate regularly (at least twice a month), and still fewer identify service as a principal commitment. At Warren Wilson, everyone is committed to service. Why else would anyone attend a college that requires it?

The work requirement, which holds students accountable for everything from whether the walks get shoveled to whether food gets on the table, accomplishes several things at once. Students learn usable skills; they cease to take for granted the myriad processes and plain hard work that go on in other places behind the scenes to support the life of a college; and the college's willingness to depend on them for vital services—i.e., to treat them as adults—tends to draw from them adult behavior.

All of this probably wouldn't work without the principle of equality that infuses so much of the campus life at Warren Wilson. Lucretia Woodruff, a 1989 graduate, reflects that the only hierarchical feature she can recall is the distribution of jobs, in which first-year students get last pick. Otherwise, she says, faculty (almost half of whom live on campus), administrators, and students operate most of the time as a single community, all dedicated to the mission of the college: to combine "academics, work, and service in a learning community committed to environmental responsibility, cross-cultural understanding, and the common good."[45] And because faculty all live on campus and remain engaged, that commitment is alive seven days a week. Without question, the Warren Wilson student body is to some extent self-selected. Those who choose to attend a college that requires work and service are likely to be at least somewhat purpose-driven before they even enroll. But student comments repeatedly credit the Triad with developing in them a balance of work, service, and intellectual life.[46]

As the wife of the director of the Bowdoin Outing Club, Lucretia Woodruff has an intimate knowledge of a very different college from the one from which she graduated. In some ways, Bowdoin and Warren Wilson have much in common: they're both small, both are committed to academic excellence in the liberal arts tradition, and both identify service as a focus of their mission. (At Bowdoin, the mantra is "the common good.") But there the resemblance ceases. Lucretia recalls visiting her then-future husband when he was a student at Bowdoin and being surprised at how little students did for themselves. Of course, she was witnessing the norm—it was *her* experience that was unusual. Not surprisingly, the current Bowdoin students who remind Lucretia most of the Warren Wilson students with whom she went to school are the student interns she and her husband employ on their farm not far from Bowdoin. She comments now that the fact that everyone at Warren Wilson worked and served seemed to produce a community of unusually mature, assured, and self-reliant students—people with a combination of intellectual depth and practical ingenuity.

Not every school, of course, is prepared to place work and service on an equal footing with the academic enterprise. Few at this point are willing to make students even peripherally responsible for their multi-million dollar plants, and those that emphasize service are likely to continue to do so through persuasion rather than by requirement. Nevertheless, on the basis of this purely anecdotal and intuitive snapshot, Warren Wilson's Triad does seem to result in uncommon maturity and responsibility in its students and to produce something approaching the purposeful community of scholars—even on the weekends—that seems so elusive elsewhere. I should note that comments from current Warren Wilson students indicate some disappointment with the level and intensity of the academic program, suggesting that perhaps the Triad has gotten a little out of balance. We can only imagine the institution that would result from a combination of the academic rigor of Princeton or Bowdoin and Warren Wilson's ethic of work, service, and collegiality.

There is one respect in which a great many American colleges and universities have had some success in stretching their students toward maturity, success on which they could profitably build. In response in part to legal requirements and in part to their own commitments, most colleges seek diversity of all kinds in their admission processes—geographic, racial, ethnic, and national. In addition, most admission officers attempt to ensure that their student bodies include the requisite number of violinists, actors, singers, football players, pole-vaulters, debaters, poets, and physicists. Though any intentional preference with respect to sexual orientation would be illegal, random selection in that category guarantees diversity.

How much does all of this diversity actually affect individual students? A look at that last category, sexual orientation, suggests that the effect is fairly dramatic. In a recent study of University of Michigan students, Diana Kardia, of that university's Center for Research on Learning and Teaching, found that 1) 60-70% of students who entered with negative attitudes toward lesbians, gay men, and bisexual people and 50% who were ambivalent displayed more positive attitudes by the time they graduated; 2) personal interaction through casual acquaintance as well as close friendship was the primary catalyst of change; 3) curricular and co-curricular attention to the topic helped establish norms that, in turn, helped influence personal attitudes; and 4) fraternities and religious groups, whose exclusivity is an innate obstacle to diversity, were both notably resistant to the trends observed otherwise.[47]

If growing up is growing out of ourselves, expanding our minds and the boundaries that restrict the universe each of us perceives, then exposure to diversity is crucial, and the college years offer an unparalleled opportunity for people to break out of their shells. Of course, the fact that almost every campus is broadly diverse doesn't mean each student experiences diversity. For the vast majority, their most diverse experience by far is the randomly grouped pre-orientation programs many colleges offer. As much as many students claim to value the variety of students they get to know in those groups, most of them gravitate from that moment on to groups of students very much like themselves. That's not surprising—most of us are attracted to like-minded people who confirm our way of seeing the world. They make us feel good, but they rarely help us grow—and therein lies the perniciousness of selective social organizations like fraternities and sororities. For all the good they claim, such organizations always seek some form of homogeneity. What other rationale is there for social selectivity? While they serve the purpose of forming social bonds among people initially attracted to one another as friends, they also reinforce their members' insularity. Walls that exclude are as high from the inside as they are from the outside, and the danger for the insiders is to become decreasingly aware of and ultimately uninterested in any way out, failing to grasp the extent to which social exclusivity arrests them emotionally and intellectually, wallowing in their own apparent worthiness, and, like over-watered plants, drowning in self-satisfaction.

Colleges eager to help students become adults will need to become far more intentional about exploiting all of that diversity to which they lay claim. They need to do all they can to coax students out of their comfort zones, where little learning happens. They need, in short, to make their students uncomfortable, and that begins with helping students recall that comfort was never their highest aspiration. Colleges that do less are simply wasting their students' time and money.

Education's goal is growth, and we grow when we learn more about ourselves and those around us. That's why American colleges have always placed so much emphasis on what goes on outside as well as inside the classroom. Those experiences that stretch us, that expose what we thought were our limits while perhaps revealing new ones, help us refine who we are, how we respond to the challenges before us, how we relate to others, and what we really care about. The traditional student classroom experience isn't enough; after all, students work only for themselves. That's why many students become depressed and unfocused. They cease to know why they're doing what they're doing because working for themselves becomes inherently unfulfilling. And that's why service, both on and off campus, is so often the key to transforming student motivation. Knowing that someone else depends on them encourages them to rise to that responsibility, and by logical extension, it frequently helps them to discover how much they depend on others. At the same time, they come to realize that the world is a lot larger than the very narrow slice of it in which they've been living.

These achievements are rarely articulated as requirements of a baccalaureate degree—but they ought to be. How else are college graduates to be ready for the world they are entering and which has so very much at stake in their being properly prepared?

CHAPTER 12

Building an Adult Society

What if children ran the world? No doubt, there are some romantics who assume a world run by children would be just this side of paradise. One suspects such people don't have children. William Golding, author of the classic flight of fancy on this subject, *Lord of the Flies*, was surely closer to the mark. We're back at the distinction between "child-like," which takes some maturity to maintain in the face of adversity, and "childish," which brings out the worst in us. What, then, would the world look like if it were run by children? Given children's innate self-centeredness, the best we could probably expect is a Darwinian culture in which the bullies would hold most of the power, in which the vast majority of the world's resources would be concentrated in the hands of a few, in which war were waged with increasing ferocity to protect the power of the few at the substantial expense of the many, in which dictators hung onto power regardless of the cost, in which people paid attention to science only when it told them what they wanted to hear, in which disappearing resources were used as if their supply were unlimited, in which many of those in power acted as though they were immortal while treating as trivial the lives of those they should be serving.

Oh, wait. That *is* what the world looks like.

I am not a pessimist. But it's hard for even an out-and-out optimist with any degree of realism to be bullish these days about the prospects for the human species. We have managed to come up with such an astonishing array of ways of doing ourselves in as a species that the odds really do appear to be against us. Our hope lies in what, over the long history of our species, are the two most adult decisions we've ever made: to form families to care for one another, and to form communities to offer the services our families can't provide. What marks those as distinctively *adult* decisions is that they forced us to choose to relinquish personal power in favor of the common good, and such a choice could have been made only by people who, to return to the definition of adulthood suggested in the Introduction, accepted the limits of their mortality and understood they weren't the center of the universe.

The root of our world's trouble is in the fragility of family and community. Family, of course, can take many shapes—extended, nuclear, single-parent, and so on. Children may be raised, as was the current President of the United States, by their grandparents, or by two mothers, two fathers, an aunt or uncle, or foster parents. That families are developing new forms in response to the expanding acceptance of non-traditional relationships is not at issue here; non-traditional families can provide for those within them as effectively as traditional families. What is at issue is the widespread breakdown of permanent domestic arrangements that are meant to ensure the ongoing care of all of their members, and especially children. Without such families, no matter what their shape, children founder. Moreover, the children of disintegrated families tend to have poor models for creating families of their own as well as no idea of either how to support the larger community or why they should. I've reflected in earlier chapters about building relationships and families. What I want to focus on now is citizenship.

Even a cursory glance at the political landscape in America provides more than sufficient evidence that Americans are largely disengaged as citizens. If, in 1961, they were stirred by President Kennedy's clarion call to "ask not what your country can do for you," now, to the contrary, that question seems to be the only one they bother to ask: "What's the government done for me lately?" That, in a democracy, they *are* the government seems to escape many Americans. True, people feel disenfranchised in a system that permits wealthy interests to buy candidates and votes. But many have simply stopped worrying about anyone but themselves, legitimately concerned that if they don't, no one else will, content to live in a nation that calls itself the wealthiest in the world and yet allows 22% of its children to live in poverty. [48] In December, 2009, according to a Rasmussen

Reports survey, 65% of Americans wanted smaller government and fewer services.[49] Of course, when anyone dares to parse that observation, it turns out Americans favor fewer services only as long as there's no reduction in the services they themselves use. Witness the healthcare debate, in which everyone was for less government until the subject was Medicare. In the summer of 2010, during town hall meetings about health care and the economy, one voter uttered the immortal cry that surely garnered the Clueless Irony Award: "Keep your government hands off my Medicare!"

We seem afflicted by a selfish acquisitiveness that countervails our communitarian impulses. It's tempting, of course, to blame the economy and the fact that so many people are in dire straights. Counterintuitive as it seems, however, our problem may be not our poverty but, rather, our prosperity. In his recent book *Boomerang*, a book about the global sovereign debt crisis, Michael Lewis, one of my favorite authors, introduced me to the work of psychiatrist and UCLA professor Peter Whybrow. Exploring in his own book, *American Mania: When More Is Not Enough,*[50] why it is that Americans, in particular, are so conflicted about their willingness to commit to community, he observes that, as human beings, we are hard-wired for scarcity but, as Americans, surrounded by abundance. That's true even for poor Americans, for whom constant reminders of the affluence of so many of their fellow citizens are impossible to escape. It is hardly surprising that, for rich and poor alike, wealth becomes a goal in itself—not what wealth can buy, but wealth in itself. How much wealth? As Rockefeller said, "a little bit more." We find it difficult to shed the competitiveness that scarcity brings out in us even when scarcity ceases to be an issue. But surely nothing more clearly marks true maturity than the ability to control the instinctive impulse to compete in favor of a commitment to the common good, which requires an act of the will. The formation of societies and the governments by which they are regulated depends on such a commitment.

Because we've failed to such an extent as citizens to take responsibility for government, we have lost our grip on the very nature of democracy. Despite the razor-thin margins of so many recent elections, especially the Presidential election of 2000, people still don't think their vote counts for much. We are bombarded with political talk, but much of it is so bombastic and shallow that it sheds little real light on the issues. One would like to be cheered by the increasing time it takes Americans to make up their minds about elections and the fact that more and more of them identify themselves as independents. But the reason may not be open-mindedness; more likely, they're simply not getting around to considering the issues. That this is likely true is attested by the speed with which large swaths of the American populace frequently move from one side to another on an issue. Though we are loath to admit it, we may no longer be a people motivated by deep-seated and well-understood principles. Even those who consider themselves "principled" are quite ready to yield basic American rights, as long as they're someone else's rights. The Bill of Rights, for example, has taken something of a beating in the War on Terror, with few Americans noting that if the terrorists succeed in getting us to yield the nation's soul, they will have won. All of this may betray a cultural unwillingness to grow up—to overcome whatever selfishness and apathy might prevent us from attending to the well being of the community.

Democratic government is a compact among individuals to join forces for the common good. But our commitment to the common good seems to be eroding. As Americans come of age, many seem to look upon their role not as agents for the American promise of opportunity for all but as contestants in a cutthroat arena whose chief task is to figure out how to win—or, at least, how not to lose. As a society, we seem deeply in touch with the pioneer tradition of rugged individualism, but we've largely forgotten the equally American spirit of barn-raisings, in which pioneer neighbors climbed over their split-rail fences to help one another. The essence of "government of the people, by the people, and for the people" is simply the spirit of barn-raisings writ large. Just as family is the quintessence of relationship, so is community the quintessence of service.

How, then, shall we re-engage our citizens? How do we remind people as they come of age what it means to be an American? How do we develop in them an impulse toward citizenship?

It turns out we're already doing this fairly successfully with a small percentage of young Americans. Those who join the military dedicate themselves to serving the nation. Joining a group of men and women to whom they develop loyalty and from whom they receive as much in kind, they discover the value of being an essential part of a cause greater than themselves. Not infrequently, raw recruits find in the military opportunities for training that make them both more productive citizens and better job candidates when they leave the military.

Why not expand this model into a universal public service program? Not just military service, but a whole array of service opportunities, of which the military would be just one option—e.g., rebuilding the nation's infrastructure; expanding conservation efforts; assisting in the delivery of health care; providing teaching and mentoring for the millions of American children who are barely getting by; offering improved recreation opportunities; augmenting public art, music, theater, and dance; expanding the Peace Corps and reaching out internationally in other ways. The mind reels with possibilities. Some programs, like the arts and the Peace Corps, would clearly call for special skills and selectivity, as Officer Candidate School does now. Others, like road building and repair, would require fewer specialized skills. Goodness knows, the need is there, and it's difficult to imagine a better targeted stimulus plan, as this one would provide job training and work for the segment of the population with the highest unemployment rate. We do have models, of course, in the Works Progress Administration and Civilian Conservation Corps of the New Deal. If we can mount a military force to protect us from armed attack, can we not also build a civilian force to protect us from the attack of ignorance, disease, cultural malaise, and even the rust and rot of our infrastructure?

Most important, the requirement of service from every American would engage our citizens at the grass roots in the enterprise of building our nation for the future. Each of them would be able to point to something he or she accomplished on behalf of the national community. And each would have been exposed to the maturing influence of participation in a higher cause than self-promotion. This is what citizens do.

I would propose requiring all Americans to begin their commitment some time between their 18th and 25th birthdays. Some would choose to complete service before college or take time off to meet the requirement, while others might wait until after graduation or even after postgraduate fellowships. The flexibility with respect to age and experience would provide the program with potential leaders and would allow young people to pursue opportunities with which this program might otherwise interfere.

Of course, the not-inconsiderable ancillary benefit would be the increased average age and maturity of our campus populations. Even now, most university administrators are pleased to defer the entrance of students who choose to take a year to immerse themselves in another culture, or do research, or assist in a service project, recognizing that such students are likely to contribute refreshing leadership and maturity once they matriculate. Indeed, Princeton has recently started "Bridge Year," in which students postpone enrollment to take advantage of the opportunities the program offers for travel, research, and service. While Bridge Year serves just two-dozen students a year and is still in its infancy, those who have participated are already bringing a leavening effect to the campus community. Even those students in a national service program who choose to complete their service after college would benefit by association with those who complete the requirement prior to entering. The more adult population would likely be more inclined toward a level of collegiality with the faculty that could, in itself, transform the learning experience.

Certainly, what I'm proposing is complex. The current number of US military personnel is roughly 2.3 million. A required public service program would embrace at least 4 million people. How do you prevent a service program from actually increasing the unemployment rate? Can we employ both the vision and the pragmatism, both of which are American hallmarks, to identify needs both in this country and abroad that could benefit from efforts of public servants that wouldn't duplicate the work of current laborers? The cost and logistics of such a program, to be sure, are nothing short of mindboggling. But so are the potential benefits to both individuals and society at large, even beyond the United States. A program like this could be transformative in a multitude of ways. Indeed, if 45% of our current college students are essentially wasting the enormous sums being poured into tuition, room, and board by their parents, financial aid programs, and the federal government, then a program that substantially improved the value of that investment would be worth quite a lot. In fact, if a universal service plan led even a modest percentage of young people to postpone their college plans, thus increasing the age, experience, and general maturity of America's campus populations, the resulting change in the sense of purpose and general tone of campus life might well be quite dramatic.

I'm not sufficiently deluded to think that, in the midst of a deep recession with a trillion-dollar debt, Americans will race to offer what would be our biggest government program after Medicare and Social Security. And both of those are partially paid for by targeted taxes, while, to the contrary, I have no suggestions about how to fund a public service plan beyond whatever growth in the economy such a program might be expected to produce. But it's time to stop pretending we as a nation aren't already paying a steep price not only for the unacceptable rate of unemployment for young people (16.5% for 20-24-year-olds in 2009; over 27% for African Americans in that age group)[51] but also for the disaffection of so many Americans for government of any sort.

If we don't address that disaffection, it's hard to see how we will maintain a democratic society. Public service is a hands-on, existential means of engaging people and institutions, and it is an effective way to help our young people grow up. By failing to ask anything of them beyond taxes as they enter the world of adults, we fail to help them understand what citizenship really means; we aren't holding them accountable for their responsibility for others—and not just Americans, of course. As citizens of the world, we bear responsibility to and for our fellow citizens across the globe as well as for the earth that supports life itself. To be an adult is to recognize and accept that responsibility.

As they survey their own opportunities, young people searching for their vocations do well to consider their broader roles as citizens. While it's easy to become stuck in a longing gaze at the horizon, asking the question, "What am I going to do with my life?," it is possible instead to ask, "How can I be useful right now?" A quicker answer may be available that need not interfere with the search for something more permanent. It may pay nothing (in dollars, at least), and probably won't be an ideal fit. But escaping from the trap of self-preoccupation and doing something for someone else is a way to become more energetic and more self-assured, and might even lead to something else. Volunteering won't resolve all anxiety about the future, but it is a way of shifting focus—and it certainly beats sitting around doing nothing. In other words, in the absence of a Public Service Program, it's possible to create a one-person public service program—or, better yet, link up with friends, employed or unemployed, to offer a necessary service. Local religious congregations or welfare organizations can offer suggestions for what to do. Every community needs volunteers.

Robert Bellah and his colleagues remind us in *Habits of the Heart* of the alienating effects of radical individualism, that "being an individual—being one's own person—does not entail escaping our ties to others, and that real freedom lies not in rejecting our social nature but in fulfilling it in a critical and adult loyalty, as we acknowledge our common responsibility to contribute to the wider fellowship of life."[52] One of the reasons young people searching for vocation often arrive at an unsatisfactory destination is their failure to factor in a commitment to their communities, be they family, friends, neighbors, countrymen, or even fellow human beings across the globe. We are by nature social animals, whose fulfillment in life is impossible in isolation from those around us. As noted earlier, our very identities are bound inextricably, for better or worse, with everyone we've touched, and everyone who has touched us. Indeed, touching and being touched might just be the most distinctive feature of what it is to be human. Adulthood is the full realization of the web of relationships that comprise who we are, and the way we attain it is to immerse ourselves fully in the world of those relationships, relinquishing the power of personal prerogative in favor of that uniquely liberating power we attain only through complete vulnerability, the gift we gain from giving, the sense of self that comes to life only as we willingly lose ourselves in commitment to others. That capacity isn't simply the basis for a healthy marriage or a happy family; it's the very heart of the good society.

We come into the world believing that all the people around us are here to serve us. But it turns out that the opposite is in fact true: we're here to serve them. Not only is that how we achieve the common good; it is also how we grow into our full identities.

Chapter 13

So What Does It Mean to Be an Adult?

I suspect most of us once dreamed of being heroes—maybe even superheroes. Of course, that's a dream destined for failure for the vast majority of us, and when it comes to superheroes, all of us. By adolescence, those of us who haven't yet won Olympic gold or dashed into a burning building to save a baby are stuck with an image of ourselves that falls well short of the heroic. Part of the very nature of adolescence is our often painful awareness of what flawed creatures we are.

It is during adolescence that tragedy first comes alive for most of us. As we come to grips with the realization that, because of our limitations, outright heroism is not our lot, we identify with the tragic hero, who at least achieves some degree of grandeur before his own hubris brings him crashing down. If the drama of it all is enticing, the end result is certainly not, at least with respect to the hero, whose ultimate fate is decidedly lacking in heroism.

There is one other type of hero that beckons our identification, and though this model is a remarkably accurate reflection of most of us, our pride leads us to resist it. I speak, of course, of the comic hero.

Nearly 40 years ago, I attended a lecture given by a friend, the late Fontaine Belford, then a star of the English faculty at Goucher College. The subject was the difference between the tragic and comic hero in literature. The tragic hero, she said, moves inexorably toward some metaphorical stone wall, crashing into it headlong, utterly destroying himself in the process. Brutus was the example she cited. The comic hero, on the other hand, moves just as inexorably toward a stone wall, and, like the tragic hero, crashes into it headlong. But here's the difference: after collapsing in a heap, the comic hero gets up unsteadily, and, though a little worse for the wear, climbs over the stonewall to head off inexorably for the next stonewall, crashing into it headlong, and so on *ad infinitum*. The example was Lucy Ricardo, who could be depended on week after week to get into and out of trouble, and, thanks to reruns of *I Love Lucy*, is still doing so.

So that's all we are? Comic heroes? Surely, that's beneath our dignity. Well, the bad news is, dignity or no, the definition fits us pretty well. And the good news is, unlike tragedy, we have a chance to survive comedy. The trick is to see the heroism in our comedy even as we acknowledge the comedy in our heroism. Remember, comedy doesn't have to be funny or silly to be comic. What makes comedy comic is that it is endlessly cyclical. Of course, we'd like to think we occasionally learn something from our experiences and thus escape the cycle; but what we can't escape is the imperfection that, on the one hand, makes us human, and on the other, leads us unavoidably into that stonewall.

Humility, then, is perhaps the quintessential sign of adulthood, the humility that reminds each of us how prone to error we are, the humility that serves as an antidote to the illusion that adulthood is about getting rid of all of our warts and becoming flawless. Unfortunately, we'll never get over our imperfection. Fortunately, we don't have to.

At some level of consciousness, most of us know we'll never be perfect, but that thought can scare us into remaining children so that our capacity to be adults will never be tested. Like Peter Pan, we declare defiantly, "I won't grow up!" But unlike Peter, you and I are forced to reckon with time. In fact, the sadness he feels as Wendy's advancing maturity changes their relationship lets us know even Peter Pan isn't immune.

Growing up is a bit like marine boot camp, which is meant simultaneously to help people learn what they're made of and cut them down to size. Some, unfortunately, seem never to make it to boot camp. Not all reach their twenties with a good grasp of what they're made of. They may have been tested to death, but they still have no idea of what's distinctive about them, the extent of their limits and capabilities, or even what they really care about. Their fear of failing may have kept them from pushing the envelope at all.

Yet right alongside the fear that they may not succeed is the illusion that everything is possible, an illusion that the best of parents in places like the United States seek to plant front-and-center in the psyches of their children from the time they begin to understand language. "Dream your dreams, " we tell them. "You can be anything you want to be." Part of growing up is the destruction of that illusion, for it is plainly not the case that everything is possible. Some young people experience that as a rude awakening, even a betrayal. But disillusionment that not everything is possible need not blind them to myriad possibilities before them.

I realized my third day of college that my shaky hands ruled out the architecture career I'd been planning for several years. (A career in neuro-surgery was out, too, but fortunately I'd never entertained any ambitions there.) It was a tough moment of truth—but life was hardly over. There were still at least a few things I could do.

Our possibilities are limited in part, of course, by the necessity of making choices. Robert Frost says it poignantly:[53]

> Two roads diverged in a yellow wood,
> And sorry I could not travel both
> And be one traveler....

Here is the real moment of truth—not the one in which we cast off our illusions, but the one in which we take responsibility for the direction of our lives. Yet how do we make such a decision? The somewhat ambiguous last stanza of *The Road Not Taken* may not improve our confidence:

> I shall be telling this with a sigh
> Somewhere ages and ages hence:
> Two roads diverged in a yellow wood, and I—
> I took the one less traveled by,
> And that has made all the difference.

Most people focus on the last two lines. But that sigh has always given me pause. Amidst competing advice to conform and to march to our own drummers, it's impossible to take any path without wondering what you're missing by not taking another, or whether the one you're taking will lead ultimately to a dead-end. Nothing is more flawed about our natures than our inability to predict the future. And yet probably nothing makes life more exciting.

That we can make choices at all is what makes being grown-ups possible. But choices are scary precisely because they force us to make predictions that we know stretch us beyond our capacities. No matter how rich, smart, talented, and powerful we may be, our predictions are at best about what is probable, not what is definite. Sooner or later, everyone stands at that fork in the road, most of us a lot more than once, forced to decide one way or the other with no assurance of the outcome either way, no longer deluded that everything is possible because, manifestly, we can't go both ways at once.

I owe my good friend novelist Paul Watkins the insight that what scares some people about becoming adults is their fear that adulthood will somehow set them in stone, unable to change, locked in place by the choices they have made. Have you ever noticed how hard it is to get teenagers to close a door (except, of course, the ones that keep their parents out of their bedrooms)? Are they just keeping their options open?

We need to help young people understand that the only thing that makes adulthood rigid is our reluctance to revisit our choices. Our options tend to be far more constrained by the limits of our vision and courage than by our lack of ability or opportunity. So many possibilities exist today that didn't just a generation or two ago. Fifty years ago, people were expected to choose their life's career by the time they left college. Today's college graduates can reasonably expect to have several careers. The road not taken now may be one rejoined later. More than likely, there's a road in their future that is, at present, completely off the map. Choices they make today will certainly close some doors, but they will open others, and the universe of possibilities, if not limitless, still nevertheless exceeds their imagination.

Growing up doesn't guarantee success, which depends on a combination of talent, commitment, and timing. Coming to terms with what talent we do and don't have is a required reality test for all of us. No matter how much I admire Vladimir Horowitz's ability to sit on the stage at Lincoln Center and knock out a Rachmaninoff concerto, following in his footsteps is just not in my future. We can improve on talent, but to some extent, that's a given, or not. Our level of commitment, on the other hand, is within our control. Since some people make it look so easy, those watching from the sidelines often fail to appreciate the down-and-dirty hard work success requires of most people. And while timing certainly seem to involve luck, or fate, or some combination of the two, we do have within our power the capacity for opportunism, a quality frequently denigrated, open as it is to abuse, but which, at its best, is simply the willingness to make the most of the gifts of the moment. Most successful people make a good deal of their own timing, taking control of events where they can rather than simply leaving them to chance. If you write to a busy CEO, don't simply say, "I look forward to hearing from you." Say instead, "I'll call you next week to follow up on this letter."

There's a third goal of marine boot camp after cutting people down to size and showing them what they're worth. Marine recruits need to be taught how to become contributing members of a mutual enterprise. So do emerging adults. Whether in marriage, family, community, society, the nation, or the world, we live in relationship to others, to whom we bear responsibility and upon whom we must learn to depend. Collaboration is the most adult of behaviors—the capacity to offer the best each of us can on behalf of the good of all. We aren't always face-to-face with the people with whom we collaborate. In fact, as citizens of the world, we will never meet 99.9% of our fellow collaborators. The composer may know few of his listeners, and the painter, few of her viewers. I hope there will be many more readers of this book than I can possibly meet. Each of us is called to do what we can in collaboration with those we know and those we don't to add value to life. This troubled world of ours cries out for that gift from each of us, and none of us is exempt. It's not just a matter of responsibility, though; it is in the web of our relationships that we establish, finally, who we are.

It turns out that we've had it backwards. People don't suddenly become adults as they move out of the house, get a job, marry, or become parents. To the contrary, it is *because* they are adults that people live and work responsibly, have lasting marriages, and become nurturing parents. It is because they are adults that they take citizenship seriously, become activists for the causes they care about, and work to empower those who struggle. Is there any more adult question than, "How can I help?" Anyone can ask it, regardless of age or station. Most of us do ask it from time to time. But if, for you, it's become second nature, chances are you're an adult. That may be true, by the way, even if you don't *feel* entirely like an adult. Most people don't feel like adults until their parents have died, but most of us can't afford to wait until then to *behave* like adults. To some extent, then, we become adults from the outside in, and though that may seem a tad dishonest, sometimes it's necessary for our behavior to lead our spirits, rather than the other way around. Like love, growing up is, at least in part, an act of the will—even when the spirit isn't willing.

Of course the ultimate sign of adulthood is our acceptance of responsibility for what we do. The passive voice is the child's way out—also, it's worth noting, the politician's. The child says, "It got broken." The politician says, "Mistakes were made." The adult says, "I blew it." It is our nature to want to avoid mistakes, but it's equally natural for us to make them. Unlike children, adults know they aren't likely to get away with very much. Moreover, they've had enough experience with screwing up to be less afraid of having done so.

We all prefer respect to scorn, but where we go astray is in our assumption that people don't respect people who make mistakes. Yes, we all prefer competence to incompetence. But what we don't respect is people who make mistakes and dissemble about them. And since everyone makes mistakes, the choice is to claim them honestly or lie. Of course, it helps to be forgiving, because only those who practice forgiveness truly believe anyone else does. And since everyone makes mistakes and we will all therefore inevitably be subject to them, forgiveness can save us a great deal of pain and bitterness. But forgiveness is tough when we place too much value on being right. Most people who have difficulty forgiving others have at least as much trouble forgiving themselves. Like it or not, though, prone to error as we all are, none of us can escape the need both to forgive and to be forgiven.

It comes down to our stubborn and all-too-often unmet need to be right. Being right is pretty satisfying; but being loved for admitting you're wrong is even better—and that's one of those secrets you only discover as an adult.

It's not about age. A few of the most adult people I know are children, and more of the most childish people I know are grownups. It's finally about character. Eleanor Roosevelt once wrote, "People grow through experience if they meet life honestly and courageously. This is how character is built."[54] She might as easily have said, "This is how adults are built." Growing up is neither easy nor painless, but there isn't one of us that can't do it. Honesty about our limits and the courage to share the world with others is really all that's required.

ACKNOWLEDGMENTS

This book owes a good deal to a great many people, most of whom I cannot name here. During its writing, it seemed nearly every conversation I had was about growing up, and many of those contributed, sometimes subtly and sometimes quite directly, to the book's content. I am grateful to everyone who has been willing to be part of such conversations.

I owe a special debt of gratitude to two people, without whom *Growing Up* would not have been born, let alone grown up. For at least a decade, my good friend Howard Greene, himself an oft-published author, has pestered me with the question, "When are you going to write a book?" Over a Thanksgiving Weekend cup of coffee, I finally vowed to take him seriously. The other is Philip Glotzbach, president of Skidmore College, whose throwaway remark on a Parents Weekend impelled me to put pen to paper (or, rather, fingers to keyboard).

Early in the book's gestation, I received an email from Douglas Barry, whom I have yet to meet face-to-face as of this writing, asking whether I'd like an extra set of editorial eyes, which I quickly and gratefully accepted. Douglas has read the manuscript at every stage, injecting intelligent, incisive, yet supportive criticism and keeping me on track, at some stages believing in the project more than I did. I can't overstate his inestimable help, nor can I adequately express my thanks.

A good many friends, colleagues, and others have previewed the manuscript, and some have been good enough to offer comments, all of which I have considered, and many of which have found their way in one form or another into the text. I am particularly indebted to two friends, novelists Douglas Kennedy and Paul Watkins, both of whom provided encouragement and sound advice. To the long list of others, including especially

Walter Burrage, Rick Chrisman, Tim Foster, Sam Hansen, Steven Hill, Emily Holland, Charley Mitchell, Randy Nichols, Chris Park, Tom Powel, Dan Rosenberg, Will Schwalbe, Anne Sherwood, Arthur Strasburger, Carla Sullwold, and Lucretia Woodruff, I offer my appreciation for your help.

Finally, my profound thanks to Justin, Hilary, and Taylor, my children, who've taught me more in just over a quarter of a century about growing up than I sometimes wanted to know, and who gracefully refrained from editing my stories about them; and, of course, most of all to Carrie, my partner in the never dull, sometimes frustrating, ever interesting, and altogether consuming enterprise of parenting. As we've grown up together, she's usually outpaced me. But adulthood is less a destination than an ongoing adventure, and the path both to it and through it a spiral, not a straight line, a continuous revelation of fresh insights. To be sure, we encounter some of our old psychic motifs again and again, but each time from a new perspective. And in that, we're blessed, for while it's not necessary to spend half our lives becoming adults, the goal isn't simply to get there; it's to keep growing.

FCS

Brunswick, Maine
December, 2011

END NOTES

1   Hall, Grant Stanley, *Adolescence: Its Psychology and Its Relations to Phyiology, Anthropology, Sociology, Sex, Crime, Religion and Education* (Prentice-Hall, Englewood Cliffs, NJ, 1904).

2   Erikison, Erik, *Identity, Youth, and Crisis* (W. W. Norton & Company, New York, 1968).

3   *High School Graduation Rates in Washington and the United States: A Long-Run View* (Washington Institute of Public Policy, Olympia, WA, March 2005).

4   Rampell, Catherine, "College Enrollment Rate at Record High," in *The New York Times,* April 28, 2010.

5   Arum, Richard and Josipa Roksa, *Academically Adrift: Limited Learning on College Campuses,* (The University of Chicago Press, Chicago, 2011).

6   *Median Age at First Marriage: 1890-2010,* retrieved from http://www.infoplease.com/ipa/A0005061.html.

7   "Transition to Adulthood," Volume 20, Number 1, Spring, 2010, from *The Future of Children,* a collaboration of the Woodrow Wilson School of Public and International Affairs at Princeton University and the Brookings Institution, Princeton, NJ.

8   Intercensal Estimates of the Resident Population by Sex, Race, and Hispanic Origin for the United States: April 1, 2000 to July 1, 2010, US Census Bureau, retrieved from http://www.census.gov/popest/national/asrh/NC-EST2009-sa.html.

9 Coffin, William Sloan, in a sermon attended by the author at Battell Chapel, Yale University, New Haven, Connecticut in 1971.

10 Kushner, Harold, *When Bad Things Happen to Good People*, (Random House, New York, 1981).

11 Henig, Robin Marantz, "What Is It About 20-Somethings," in *The New York Times Magazine*, August 22, 2010.

12 Arnett, Peter, *Emerging Adulthood: The Winding Road from the Late Teens through the Twenties* (Oxford University Press, New York, 2004), p. 55.

13 *Ibid.*

14 Erikson, Erik, *Identity, Youth and Crisis* (W. W. Norton & Company, New York, 1968), p. 157.

15 Arnett, op. cit., p. 8.

16 Henig, op. cit.

17 *Ibid.*

18 *Ibid.*

19 Siegel, Bernie, *Love, Medicine, and Miracles,* (Harper & Row, New York, 1986).

20 Buber, Martin, *I and Thou* (Charles Scribner's Sons, New York, 1958).

21 "Teen Homicide, Suicide, and Firearm Deaths," in *Child Trends* (2010), retrieved from http://www.childtrendsdatabank.org/?q=node/124.

22 Schulz, Kathryn, *Being Wrong: Adventures in the Margin of Error* (Ecco/Harper Collins, New York, 2010), p. 164.

23 Lee, Harper, *To Kill a Mockingbird (HarperCollins, New York,*1960).

24 Ferriss, Timothy, Interview at the Commonwealth Club of California, Sam Francisco, CA January 6, 2011 (broadcast on National Public Radio).

25 Princeton University web site, January 19, 2011, retrieved from http://www.princeton.edu/main/news/archive/S29/53/88I91/index.xml?section=topstories.

26 Princeton University web site, September 19, 2011, retrieved from http://www.princeton.edu/main/news/archive/S31/64/67K05/.

27   Brooks, David, "It's Not About You," in *The New York Times*, May 30, 2011

28   Kristof, Nicholas and Sheryl WuDunn, *Half the Sky: Turning Oppression into Opportunity for Women Worldwide* (Vintage Books, a Division of Random House, Inc., New York, 2010).

29   Karlsson-Sjögren, Åsa, *Männen, kvinnorna och rösträtten : medborgarskap och representation 1723-1866* ("Men, women and the vote: citizenship and representation 1723–1866") (in Swedish), retrieved from http://en.wikipedia.org/wiki/Women's_suffrage#cite_note-elections.org.nz-3.

30   Elections New Zealand, retrieved from http://www.elections.org.nz/study/education-centre/history/votes-for-women.html.

31   *Sexual Violence: Facts at a Glance*, Spring, 2008 (US Centers for Disease Control, Atlanta, GA).

32   Sampson, Rana, *Acquaintance Rape of College Students,* Problem-Oriented Guides for Police, Problem-Specific Guide Series, No. 17, p. 3 (Community Oriented Policing Services, US Department of Justice, Washington, DC).

33   Lasch, Christopher, *The Culture of Narcisism: American Life in an Age of Diminishing Expectations*, (W. W. Norton & Company, Inc., New York, 1979).

34   De Toqueville, Alexis, *Democracy in America*, Volume Two, Section I, Chapter I, (Saunders and Otley, London, 1840).

35   Bowles, Richard N., *What Color Is Your Parachute?* (Ten-Speed Press, Berkeley, 2011).

36   Buchholz, Esther Schaler, "The Call of Solitude," *Psychology Today*, January 1, 1998.

37   "How many North Americans Attend Religious Services (and How Many Lie About Going)?," retrieved from http://www.religioustolerance.org/rel_rate.htm (Ontario Consultants on Religious Tolerance, August 10, 2010).

38   Roberts, Sam, "Most Children Still Live in Two-Parent Homes, Census Bureau Reports," *The New York Times,* February 21, 2008.

39 *College Drinking—Changing the Culture* (National Institute of Alcohol Abuse and Alcoholism, Bethesda, MD, 2010).

40 *College Alcohol Study Abstract: Alcohol Abuse and Dependence Among U.S. College Students*, Harvard School of Public Health, Cambridge, MA, 2005).

41 Sack, Kevin, "At the Legal Limit," *The New York Times*, October 29, 2008.

42 Conversation with Tim Foster, Dean of Students, Bowdoin College, Brunswick, ME, June 30, 2011.

43 Having served during my undergraduate years as head of Princeton's Orange Key Guides, I am blessed (or cursed) with an unlimited pool of nickel knowledge about Princeton that remains imbedded in my memory and therefore found it unnecessary to consult any sources for most of the factual information I've included here. Nevertheless, for those who wish to pursue Princeton's history in more detail, the best source for the 20th century is James Axtell's *The Making of Princeton University: From Woodrow Wilson to the Present*, Princeton University Press, 2006, and current information is available on Princeton's web site: www.princeton.edu.

44 My information on Warren Wilson College comes from the school's web site: www.warren-wilson.edu, from alumna Lucretia Woodruff '89, and from *Warren Wilson College 2012*, by Michael Metzler and Roxy Todd (College Prowler, Pittsburgh, PA, 2011).

45 Mission Statement, Warren Wilson College, retrieved from http://www.warren-wilson.edu/info/plan/mission.php.

46 Retrieved from http://www.warren-wilson.edu/triad/index.php.

47 Kardia, Diana, "Student Attitudes Toward Gay and Lesbian Issues: The Impact of College," in *Diversity Digest* (Association of American Colleges and Universities, Washington, DC, Summer 1998), Retrieved from http://www.diversityweb.org/digest/sm98/attitudes.html.

48 2010 Child Well-Being Index, Foundation for Child Development.

49 *America's Best Days*, Rasmussen Reports, Asbury Park, NJ, May 29, 2011.

50 Whybrow, Peter C., MD, *American Mania: When More Is Not Enough* (W. W. Norton & Company, New York, 2005).

51 Household Data Not Seasonally Adjusted Quarterly Averages, E-16: Unemployment Rates by Age, Sex, Race, and Hispanic or Latino Ethnicity, retrieved from http://www.bls.gov/web/empsit/cpseed16. pdf (Bureau of Labor Statistics, Washington, DC, 2011).

52 Bellah, Robert, *et al.*, *Habits of the Heart* (Updated Edition) (University of California Press, Berkeley, CA, 1996), p. ix.

53 Frost, Robert, *The Road Not Taken* (Henry Holt and Company, New York, 1920).

BIBLIOGRAPHY

Books and Poetry

Peter Arnett, *Emerging Adulthood: The Winding Road from the Late Teens through the Twenties* (Oxford University Press, New York, 2004)

Richard Arum and Josipa Roksa, *Academically Adrift: Limited Learning on College Campuses* (The University of Chicago Press, Chicago, 2011).

Ernest Becker, *The Denial of Death* (The Free Press, a Division of Macmillan Publishing Co., Inc., New York, 1973).

Robert Bella, Richard Madsen, William M. Sullivan, Ann Swidler, and Steven M. Tipton, *Habits of the Heart,* Updated Edition (University of California Press, Berkeley, CA, 1996)

Richard N. Bowles, *What Color Is Your Parachute?* (Ten-Speed Press, Berkeley, 2011).

Martin Buber, *I and Thou* (Charles Scribner's Sons, New York, 1958).

Esther Schaler Buchholz, *The Call of Solitude: Alonetime in a World of Attachment* (Simon & Schuster, New York, 1997).

Ralph Waldo Emerson, "Self Reliance," *Essays,* 1841.

Erik Erikson, *Identity, Youth, and Crisis* (W. W. Norton & Company, New York, 1968).

Robert Frost, *The Road Not Taken* (Henry Holt and Company, New York, 1920).

William Golding, *Lord of the Flies* (Berkley Publishing Group, a Division of Penguin Putnam Inc., New York, 1954).

Granville Stanley Hall, *Adolescence: Its Psychology and Its Relations to Phyiology, Anthropology, Sociology, Sex, Crime, Religion, and Education* (Prentice-Hall, Englewood Cliffs, NJ, 1904).

Nicholas Kristof and Sheryl WuDunn, *Half the Sky: Turning Oppression into Opportunity for Women Worldwide* (Vintage Books, a Division of Random House, Inc., New York, 2010).

Harold Kushner, *When Bad Things Happen to Good People* (Random House, New York, 1981).

Christopher Lasch, *The Culture of Narcicism: American Life in an Age of Diminishing Expectations (W. W. Norton & Company, New York, 1979).*

Harper Lee, *To Kill a Mockingbird* (HarperCollins, New York, 1960).

Kathryn Schulz, *Being Wrong: Adventures in the Margin of Error* (Ecco/HarperCollins, New York, 2010).

Bernie Siegel, *Love, Medicine, and Miracles* (Harper & Row, New York, 1986).

Alexis De Toqueville, *Democracy in America*, Volume Two (Saunders and Otley, London, 1840).

Peter Whybrow, *American Mania: When More Is Not Enough* (W. W. Norton & Company, New York, 2005).

Articles, Abstracts, and Interviews

America's Best Days, Rasmussen Reports, Asbury Park, NJ, May 29, 2011.

David Brooks, "It's Not About You," in *The New York Times*, May 30, 2011.

Esther Buchholz, "The Call of Solitude," *Psychology Today*, January 1, 1998.

College Alcohol Study Abstract: Alcohol Abuse and Dependence Among U.S. College Students, Harvard School of Public Health, Cambridge, MA, 2005).

College Drinking—Changing the Culture (National Institute of Alcohol Abuse and Alcoholism, Bethesda, MD, 2010).

Elections New Zealand, retrieved from http://www.elections.org.nz/study/education-centre/history/votes-for-women.html.

Timothy Ferriss, Interview at the Commonwealth Club of California, Sam Francisco, CA January 6, 2011 (broadcast on National Public Radio).

Timothy Foster, Dean of Student Affairs, Bowdoin College, Brunswick, ME, interviewed by the author June 30, 2011.

Robin Marantz Henig, "What Is It About 20-Somethings," in *The New York Times Magazine*, August 22, 1910.

High School Graduation Rates in Washington and the United States: A Long-Run View (Washington Institute of Public Policy, Olympia, WA, March 2005).

Household Data Not Seasonally Adjusted Quarterly Averages, E-16: Unemployment Rates by Age, Sex, Race, and Hispanic or Latino Ethnicity, retrieved from http//www.bls.gov/web/empsit/cspeed16.pdf (Bureau of Labor Statistics, Washington, DC, 2011).

"How many North Americans Attend Religious Services (and How Many Lie About Going)?," retrieved from http://www.religioustolerance.org/rel_rate.htm (Ontario Consultants on Religious Tolerance, August 10, 2010).

"Intercensal Estimates of the Resident Population by Sex, Race, and Hispanic Origin for the United States: April 1, 2000 to July 1, 2010", US. Census Bureau, retrieved from http://www.census.gov/popest/national/asrh/NC-EST2009-sa.html.

Diana Kardia, "Student Attitudes Toward Gay and Lesbian Issues: The Impact of College," in *Diversity Digest* (Association of American Colleges and Universities, Washington, DC, Summer 1998), Retrieved from http://www.diversityweb.org/digest/sm98/attitudes.html.

Åsa Karlsson-Sjögren, *Männen, kvinnorna och rösträtten : medborgarskap och representation 1723-1866* ("Men, women and the vote: citizenship and representation 1723–1866") (in Swedish), retrieved from http://en.wikipedia.org/wiki/Women's_suffrage#cite_note-elections.org.nz-3.

Randall T. Nichols, Director of Safety and Security, Bowdoin College, Brunsiwck, ME, interviewed by the author April 8, 2011.

Catherine Rampell, "College Enrollment Rate at Record High," in *The New York Times,* April 28, 2010.

Sam Roberts, "Most Children Still Live in Two-Parent Homes, Census Bureau Reports," *The New York Times,* February 21, 2008.

Kevin Sack, "At the Legal Limit," *The New York Times*, October 29, 2008.

Rana Sampson, *Acquaintance Rape of College Students,* Problem-Oriented Guides for Police, Problem-Specific Guide Series, No. 17, p. 3 (Community Oriented Policing Services, US Department of Justice, Washington, DC).

Sexual Violence: Facts at a Glance, Spring, 2008 (US Centers for Disease Control, Atlanta, GA).

Valerie Smith, Dean of the College, Princeton University, Princeton, NJ, interviewed by the author July 7, 2011.

"Teen Homicide, Suicide, and Firearm Deaths," in *Child Trends* (2010). Retrieved from http://www.childtrendsdatabank.org/?q=node/124.

"Transition to Adulthood," Volume 20, Number 1, Sping, 2010, from *The Future of Children,* a collaboration of the Woodrow Wilson School of Public and International Affairs at Princeton University and the Brookings Institution, Princeton, NJ.

Lucretia Woodruff, of Brunswick, ME, alumna of Warren Wilson College, interviewed by the author July 3, 2011.

About the Author

Frank Strasburger has devoted most of his 45-year career as a teacher and priest to young people. After teaching at some of the nation's top independent schools, he was the Episcopal Chaplain at Princeton University for more than a decade. He is cofounder and emeritus president of Princeton in Africa, which provides year-long service opportunities all over Africa for recent college graduates. Now retired, Strasburger teaches writing to high school seniors, is a mentor in a program for troubled teens, and serves on a number of nonprofit boards. The father of three grown children, he lives with his wife Carrie on the coast of Maine.